March 14/94

Susan ....

You're a winner !

Keep on developing your
untapped potential. (10%)

Successfully,
Rosalie.

Creative Innovators

CREATIVE INNOVATORS

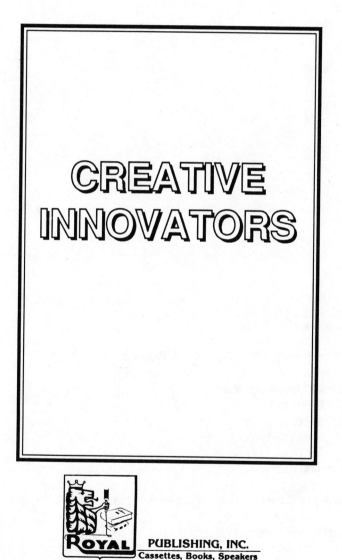

ROYAL PUBLISHING, INC.
Cassettes, Books, Speakers

Creative Innovators

Creative Innovators

© Copyright 1988 by Dorothy M. Walters

Royal Publishing, Inc
P.O. Box 1120
18825 Hicrest Road
Glendora, California 91740

Library of Congress Cataloging in Publication Date in Progress.

ISBN 0-934344-26-4

Printed in the United States of America

Infinite Variety

There's a beat in Beatles that you may not hear;
the Creator is singing it, loud and clear.

*"Study My Creation, and you will know
quintessence of genius — how ideas flow.*

*At the Heart of My atom, life's a-pound,
pulsing power ringing, 'round and 'round.*

*Open your eyes! There is not 'one way.'
My Heavens are out-pouring. Look up today.*

*Myriads of species I create.
Two hundred thousand beetles circulate!*

*I never make one type of anything—
infinite variety's the song I sing!*

*Yet of each individual, I make only one.
'You are unique,' The rhyme I hum.*

*I love ideas, so let Mine through!
I am knocking at your mind, singing now to you!*

*Let music of My spheres be your melody,
My kaleidoscope of Life… Our rhapsody!"*

- Dottie Walters

CREATIVE INNOVATORS

CONTENTS

Dr. Yoshiro NakaMats

Dr. Yoshiro NakaMats

Inventor of the floppy disk, the digital watch and 2,360 active patents, Dr. Yoshiro NakaMats is the most creative, prolific inventor on earth. His patents far exceed Thomas Edison's, who registered 1,093. The famous Japanese inventor and businesman holds the International Hall of Fame and the United States Presidential Awards.

Dr. NakaMats speaks on the "5 Tiered Pagoda of Creativity" (the title of one of his 8 best selling books in Japan). He explains the first tier is Spirit; 2nd is the Healthy Body; 3rd, Knowledge; 4th, Experience; and the 5th is the great FLASH! of the mind (reminiscent of Albert Einstein's remarks about the "leap of the mind").

Dr. Makamats' inventions include a robot named Cerebrex, and the Cerebrex Chair which enables the user to get a full night's rest in 20 minutes, and to become extremely focused for creativity. He has created special snack foods which scientifically increase the brain's ability to create. At his laboratory in Japan he has equipped a one million dollar Creative Think Tank, which he uses daily.

Dr. NakaMats, a member of the highest level Samurai family, is in great demand worldwide as a speaker. His position in Japan is equal to the Prime Minister, or a Cabinet Member. He is one of the top 100 International Speakers.

Dr. NakaMats is the originator of the World Genius Convention which is held annually each October in Tokyo. Inventors from all over the globe gather in one of the largest exhibits of new ideas on earth.

A Message on Creativity

...From Dr. Yoshiro NakaMats

Dr. NakaMats, one of the most creative innovators who has ever lived, explains his method of bringing the creative mental process into practical existence. "You are most apt to have creative thoughts when you are are in water, in your bed, or riding," he says.

"Arrange your thoughts in this way:

First, decide on your *Suji*, or *Theory.*

Second, be sure you have *Pika*, or *Fresh Ideas,* not extensions of existing ones.

Third, carefully work out your *Iki*, which means *Practicality* and *Feasibility.*"

Dr NakaMats sleeps very little. He is constantly creating new inventions and methods in his "idea factory" in Toyko Japan. This is his philosophy:

"You must use every minute of your life. If you have been given the mental potential of a six, and only use a three during your lifetime, you will die unfulfilled.

However, if you are given the potential of a six, and have pressed forward all the days, the hours, and the minutes of your life until you have reached an eight, a ten or even a twelve, you will die happy. The purpose of life is to fulfill our potential and surpass it."

Denis Waitley, Ph.D.
Denis Waitley, Inc.
P.O. Box 197
Rancho Santa Fe, CA 92067
(619) 756-4201

Denis Waitley, Ph.D.

Dr. Denis Waitley is the master when it comes to understanding self-development and high performance. He has achieved and maintained this status by thoroughly researching the principles he first revealed in "Psychology of Winning", the all-time best-selling audio cassette album on self-management.

He is one of the most sought after speakers in the world. He has few peers in the communication of complex and profound truths in easy-to-understand and interesting terms. He has shared the platform with President Ronald Reagan, Lee Iacocca, Tom Peters, Paul Harvey, Peter Drucker, Barbara Walters, Norman Vincent Peale and other leaders in their fields.

Denis Waitley has studied and counseled winners in every walk of life from top executives of Fortune 500 companies to Super Bowl champions, from our astronauts to returning POW's. He has served as a member of the United States Olympic Committee's Sports Medicine Council; has been named "Outstanding Speaker of the Year" by the Sales and Marketing Executives Association; placed into the International Speakers Hall of Fame in St. Louis; and served as a visiting scholar at the University of Southern California's College of Continuing Education. He is a graduate of the United States Naval Academy at Annapolis and holds a doctoral degree in human behavior.

He is author of numerous best-selling books on self improvement including the classic Seeds of Greatness, The Winner's Edge, The Double Win *and* The Joy of Working.

Foreword

By Denis Waitley, Ph.D.

As we enter the final decade of the 20th Century, I believe we have a tremendous opportunity for a Renaissance of Creativity. As the computer takes over many of our purely routine and mechanical functions, our time and our minds will be more available to create, indeed, to innovate. We should be able to experience interpersonal relationships based more on feelings, emotions, and spiritual love than we have in the past. Instead of passively watching television, we can actively visualize and create our own futures, in advance.

But first, we have to believe we deserve success. Then, we need to visualize and verbalize success, as if we are script writers for a TV documentary on our own lives.

Napoleon once said, "Imagination rules the world." Einstein believed that imagination is more important than knowledge, for knowledge is limited to all we now know and understand, while imagination embraces the entire world and all there ever will be to know and understand.

We human beings, with no prerecorded computer program as our lifeguide, are blessed with a creative imagination. Yet most of our awake lives are under the conscious control of our left-brain. When we are blessed with a "great idea" or "flash of insight" it seems to arrive suddenly and in a surprisingly complete form. Apparently, it was incubating unconsciously in our right-brain. Mozart and Beethoven said they heard symphonies in their heads, and had only to write them down.

One of my favorite innovators is Igor Sikorsky, who built the first four-engine airplane in 1913 in his native Russia. When it flew successfully, the left-brain critics said it would never fly high enough and far enough to be of real economic value. He proved them wrong again.

When the Communists took over, Sikorsky had to flee, as did so many creative thinkers. He arrived in the United States broke but eager to create. He went on to pioneer transoceanic commercial air travel with his Flying Clippers and in his mid-fifties developed the helicoptor, an invention his American critics said could never fly.

As an eleven-year-old boy, Sikorsky is reported to have had a dream in which he was walking along a paneled passageway, lit by soft blue lights. He dreamed he was inside a big flying ship — one that he had built himself.

About thirty years later, he was copilot on one of his big flying boats. His friend Charles Lindbergh was at the controls and Sikorsky decided to take a stretch, walking back in the passenger cabin. In a "flash of insight" he found himself walking along that paneled passageway, inside a big flying ship, lit by soft blue lights!

All you and I need to unleash our creativity is to be "whole brain thinkers." Thousands of years ago we were more emotional and intuitive. As we learned how to use tools and communicate, we developed into a left-brain society utilizing verbalization, logic and practical, step-by-step solutions to our problems. The technological progress has been staggering and we seem to have accomplished more during the past fifty years, in terms of scientific breakthroughs, than in all the previous years in our history combined.

And this is just the beginning! Now we can combine technology with caring for each other and consideration for a purpose greater than ourselves. By learning from history, we can design a future worthy of our children.

Dottie Walters, a wellspring of creativity and innovation, has brought us this marvelous anthology to enrich and stir our own powers within. Read, enjoy, relate, and innovate.

"Every age needs those who will redeem the time by living with a vision of things that are to be."
\- Adlai Stevenson

Creative Innovators

Robert B. Tucker
The Innovation Resource
P.O. Box 30930
Santa Barbara, CA 93130
(805) 682-1012

Robert B. Tucker

Robert B. Tucker makes innovation happen. His insights into why innovatiors and their companies are thriving and prospering in America's New Economy are derived from a unique source. He is the only expert to have personally sought out this nation's trendsetters for extensive, indepth interviews and analysis.

Tucker began investigating what makes innovators tick during the recession of 1982-83. As an award-winning business writer, he noticed that certain individuals and companies were apparently thriving because of changes in the U.S. and global economies, while others were being destroyed by change. To understand this phenomenon, Tucker criss-crossed America to study many of the top CEOs, entrepreneurs, managers, "Knowledge merchants" and futurists. What was it that separated the winners from the losers? The result of this study was the book Winning the Innovation Game *co-authored with Denis Waitley, which demonstrates how innovation is a systematic process of discovering and developing new opportunites based on societal and technological change.*

Robert Tucker is president of The Innovation Resource, a Santa Barbara, California firm which specializes in customized programs for executives and managers. A dynamic speaker and seminar leader, he regularly addresses major trade associations and corporations.

In addition, Tucker has appeared on such programs as Financial News Network, Window on Wall Street *and ABC's* Michael Jackson Show. *His articles on innovation appear in such publications as* INC., Esquire, Success, Omni *and* The Futurist, *and have been syndicated by the* Los Angeles Times *to over 50 newspapers. He is the author/narrator of* How to Profit From Today's Rapid Changes *(Simon & Schuster) and* How to Think Like an Innovator *(Nightingale Conant Corp.)*

Introduction

By Robert Tucker

Innovation as Rx for Mediocrity

Fantastic! That was my reaction when Dottie Walters invited me to write an introduction to this anthology of "Creative Innovators." You see, I believe the more attention we pay to creativity and innovation, the better off we'll all be. Because we must all become innovators if we want to thrive and prosper into the next century.

We've entered a new era of accelerating change, intensifying competition, and increasing complexity. This is a time full of both pitfalls and promises. If we stand idly by and do what we did yesterday, our standard of living will continue to decline. Our social and economic problems will get worse. We'll become a second-rate nation.

But if we unleash the power of innovation, we can all win!

Innovation is really a mental orientation to life; being aware, curious, open, perceptive and alert to new opportunities. It means optimistically searching for better ways of doing things. It means looking for new solutions to old problems.

The same process of problem-solving that occurs in the reasearch lab can occur in our own lives. Innovation is the act of putting ideas to work to solve problems and create opportunities — for yourself, your organization and your family. It's the act of introducing improvements into your life. It's figuring out what you really want to do next, and doing it. It's the step-by-step process of creating the life you want to lead.

My four-year study of some of America's leading innovators was an adventure I'll always remember. I felt like I was following in the footsteps of Napoleon Hill, who interviewed the innovators of his day. (He didn't call them that, but that's what they were.)

Like Hill, I too found some secrets. Perhaps the most surprising thing to me was that both the big and little breakthroughs in life all spring from curiosity, not high intelligence. If you're curious, it's going to drive you to figure out how that watch works, or what happens inside your hand, or, like Fred Smith, who founded Federal Express, why it's so hard to get packages delivered on time.

I like what Buckminster Fuller said: "There's no such thing as genius. Some of us are just less damaged than others." So many people have these "I'm not creative" tapes from their early experience, which can incapacitate them. We have to take the initiative and unravel that negative thinking and replace it with the attitude of "try anything, try everything, until something works." This is what innovators do. And it's why they are so richly rewarded.

I think that people are sold a bill of goods when they're told superficial ways to gain confidence, such as image-building or dressing for success. These things don't do much to change the fundamental person. But setting realistic goals and actually putting your ideas into action will do a lot more for bolstering self-esteem and changing the inner person.

That's because the more you do, the more "success episodes" you are bound to have. The more ideas you hatch, the more ideas you write down, the more ideas you act on, the more experiments you try, the more feedback you receive, the more "failures" you get out of the way, then the more successful you're going to become, the more in demand you'll be, the more money you'll make, the more your name will spread, the prouder your family will be, the more the good things in life will be yours, and the better off our country will be.

So now you know why I told Dottie, "Fantastic." This book is about my favorite topic. I sincerely hope it helps you break through with your biggest idea yet!

"Imagination is more important than knowledge."
\- Albert Einstein

CREATIVE INNOVATORS

Rosalie Wysocki
Wysocki & Associates Inc.
Village Offices of Sherwoodtowne
4287 Village Centre Court, Suite C
Mississauga, Ontario, Canada L4Z 1S2
(416) 848-2900

Rosalie Wysocki
Rosalie Wysocki is one of Canada's foremost motivational speakers and a leader in the field of personal development. Following 12 years as a business teacher, Rosalie spent five years in direct sales with a publishing company, winning recognition as a top professional and later as a divisional sales manager, responsible for recruiting, sales training and management development. During this time, she achieved top North American awards as a successful sales professional, manager and motivator.

In 1980, she established Wysocki & Associates Inc., a Mississauga, Ontario based Human Resource Development company which conducts in-house performance improvement programs for large and small organizations.

As a Performance Consultant, Rosalie specializes in personal motivation, goal setting, communications, positive attitude, time management, and team building. Committed to coaching people to be more effective and more productive, Rosalie is a "product of the product" she markets — personal growth and development.

Rosalie has held varied leadership positions at all community levels and is active on several community boards, as well as being an avid squash player and cyclist. She is an accomplished seminar leader, a dynamic speaker and a successful entrepreneur.

Rosalie is a member of the National Speakers' Association and travels internationally, speaking to widely diverse audiences. In 1987 she received the "Motivator of the Year" Award for Canada from Success Motivation Institute.

Developing the Creative Edge

By Rosalie Wysocki

"Winners are those individuals who in a very natural, free flowing way seem to consistently get what they want from life by providing valuable service to others. They put themselves together across the board — in their personal, professional, and community lives. They set and achieve goals that benefit others as well as themselves."
- Denis Waitley, The Winner's Edge

My personalized license plate reads BOSA-1. A gift from two colleagues, the plate reflects my mission statement, "Be Of Service Attitude." Why BOSA? Because by helping others win, we automatically win as well. The more service we render, the greater our success level and personal growth. A simple thing like a license plate can serve as a constant visual reminder of what's involved in winning!

It is my distinct pleasure to be able to share with you five key concepts encompassing proven success techniques to help you become more effective and productive both personally and professionally. I take little credit for the originality of these ideas. As a student of personal development over the past 13 years, I have experienced first-hand tremendous growth and development. Much of this personal success can be traced back to the many books, cassette tapes, speakers and seminars I have enjoyed and which I continue to pursue in the constant and progressive quest for continued self-improvement and satisfaction in life.

On...Developing a Winning Game Plan

The difference between genuinely successful people and those who merely make a living is simply this: Those who achieve have written and specific goals. Or, in the words of Denis Waitley, "Winners are people with a definite purpose in life."

Yet so many people go through life as if it's a dress rehearsal. We know the importance of planning for a trip or retirement — but we don't often realize the importance of having a game plan for our life. Knowing *what* you want and *how* you plan to go about achieving your goals is a major part of succeeding in life.

The Success Motivation Institute (SMI) programs conducted by our firm direct participants to set goals in six areas of life:

- Physical - Health
- Family - Home
- Social - Cultural
- Mental - Educational
- Spiritual - Ethical
- Financial - Career

One of the first steps in developing a winning game plan is to write a list of all the things you want to become, achieve, or experience in life. Endeavor to include items from the six key categories mentioned above.

From this "rough draft" you can begin to prioritize and write both short-and long-term goals.

It is essential to have personal and business plans and to *write* them down. Use a daily planner/ organizer with ample space and a proper set-up for the tracking of business and personal activities.

"Goals are as essential to success as air is to life," says Dr. Bill Hinson, a renowned motivational speaker. As well as short-and long-term plans, be sure to work on tangible and intangible goals. The greatest personal growth comes from setting and achieving intangible goals which require *change* of attitude and behavior.

It's important to develop a written Plan of Action in which you write *what* you plan to achieve and elaborate on *how* you intend to take action.

Winners have a game plan — losers don't even

know there's a game going on.

Winners keep score — losers don't want to know the score.

One of the best exercises to help you become more motivated and wanting to join in on the goal-setting *process* is to write a Success List. Jot down all the talents, achievements and wins you've experienced in life since early childhood to the present. Probe the six key areas of your life and write all the accomplishments you are proud to recall. Get to know your *strengths* as well as your weaknesses! To be a better goal-setter: (1)Write it; (2) Visualize it; (3) Plan it; (4) Go after it!

Another technique I find extremely helpful is to "take inventory" every six months. I retreat for a weekend and do an "inspect/expect" of my annual game plan. Doing this semi-annually enables me to regroup and re-set some of my action steps so it turns out to be a winning year all round.

Following the simple approach to planning is helpful. Plan for the year, then break the list of goals into months to be worked on and/or achieved and incorporate the required action steps into your plans. Use the Time Design System to complement this strategy.

Annual
Monthly
Weekly
Daily

Success is achieving your personal goals. The strongest statement regarding the need to set goals:

If you fail to plan, you plan to fail.

On...the Importance of a Positive Attitude

Twelve years ago I showed an acquaintance a cassette tape album I purchased on personal development. Her reply upon learning I had invested $75 in the tapes was, "You must be crazy to spend that kind of money for such nonsense!" I was devastated. Had I done a foolish thing? I analyzed her comment later and realized this person was a negative thinker who lacked the positive mental attitude necessary to appreciate the value of these tapes and was focused purely on the cost factor. Those tapes (*The Psychology of Winning* by Dr. Denis Waitley) were the first of many subsequent investments I made in my own personal development. What an incredible impact that first album of tapes had on my life! I recommend them highly to this day.

The one common denominator all successful people share is PMA (Positive Mental Attitude). Attitude is your mental mindset — your outlook on life, your habit of thinking. It's either positive or negative and it's your choice! You are not born with an attitude — you acquire it and it can be changed from negative to positive. People with PMA just naturally rise to the top in life and in an organization. It's been proven that

ATTITUDE determines ALTITUDE in life.

As a high school teacher for 12 years, I frequently observed that the students easiest to teach were not those with high I.Q.'s but those with a positive attitude. It was the same in coaching athletics — it wasn't just muscle and strength that determined a winner, but rather that unbeatable combination of attitude and desire.

Top athletes are the first to admit they focus on mental as well as physical conditioning to win at the game.

I work harder on developing and maintaining a positive mental attitude than anything else because a PMA affects your health, wealth, self-image and success.

Here are a few tips on how to keep your attitude positively conditioned:

1. Attend seminars regularly and listen carefully to top speakers and performers sharing insights on success and personal growth.

2. Take a winner out to lunch once a month. Successful people are willing to share ideas and are stimulating to be around. During the luncheon, ask questions regarding the techniques they practice, how they achieved their success, and so on. Remember: "More is caught than taught!"

3. Build a personal development library. Invest in and read books on personal development. I highly recommend starting with *The Joy of Working* by Denis Waitley, giving a 30-day system to success. There's also a gold mine of "what to" and "how to" in

the Psychology & Business Section bookshelves regarding self-improvement, motivation, and human potential. Include cassette tapes in your library for variety. Listening and learning while you drive, run or stationary cycle is an excellent way to invest time for personal development. Be sure to include a monthly subscription to a magazine such as *Success* for short reading material. Notes from speakers, seminars and courses also have a place on the library shelf. You'll be amazed how much comes back to you when you review them from time to time.

4. One of Dr. Bill Hinson's tapes gives the success formula: PMA + GOALS = SUCCESS. Guaranteed to bring you positive results!

5. Avoid being around negative people who have a disease called "stinkin' thinkin'". This is an attitudinal problem some people have and it can be catching! A person with PMA says when life gives you lemons, make lemonade!

6. Practice positive self-talk. The computer expression GIGO (Garbage In-Garbage Out) reaffirms that if we program negative thoughts (through self-talk) in our minds, we cause negative actions. Also, use positive affirmations daily and use the "act as if" principle—believe that what you're trying to achieve, to do or become has already happened.

7. And remember to P.A.C.E. yourself because **P**ositive **A**ttitude **C**hanges **E**nvironment. Success is an attitude. Get yours right!

"Your Attitude Determines Your Altitude in Life"

On...The Value of Taking Personal Inventory

I once attended a seminar at which the facilitator started by asking each participant to state what he or she had done for self-improvement during the previous year. What would you answer to that question right at this moment? Businesses take inventory prior to determining profit or loss for the year. Individuals also need to take stock of themselves to determine if they've had a winning year.

Several years ago, I had the privilege of sharing the platform with Anita Ross, then Human Resource Director of IBM Canada. Two of the excellent ideas she presented in addressing Career Strategies were:

a. Take **self-inventory** annually - preferably on your birthday. It's the ideal time for self-reflection and assessment, since it's personal and the beginning of a new year.

b. Plan to do two **significant** things in your life each year.

When assessing where you are now and planning where you want to be in one or two years' time, it is important to look at all areas of your life. The biggest challenge of all is to *keep the balance.* Take time for a personal fitness program, plan activities with your family, friends and partner, review your financial standing, develop a career path plan, maintain regular physical and health check-ups, be involved in some type of community or church project, and take courses for mental growth and maturity.

Take the time to get an overall picture of where

you are in life right now and project on paper what you expect to achieve in a successful year. Success is achieving your personal GOALS. Write a plan of action for the year which challenges you to develop more of your untapped potential.

"Know thyself!" encouraged Socrates. Take time to get to know your strengths and weaknesses.

1. Ask three people who know you well — "What is the one major thing I can do for self-improvement?" Listen, thank them honestly and then ask, "What is my greatest strength of character or personality?" You'll be surprised what you find out about yourself!

2. Plan and take time to do one meaningful thing each day.

3. Make it a daily goal to praise someone. Give recognition where duly earned. Honest praise is the psychological food we all need, employers and employees alike, parents and children alike. We've got to start giving more of it. Ask yourself everyday, "Did I praise anyone today?"

In my wallet I carry a Success Card listing my major achievements since high school days. It serves as a visual reminder of past winnings in life as well as a reminder to continue to grow and develop each year. If you're ever feeling low, just take out your card and review your accomplishments. Innovators think of creative ways to motivate themselves and are constantly on the lookout for new ideas — despite the fact that change is almost always a part of the process of growth and development.

Occasionally, I ask seminar participants to tell us

what they've done in the past year for growth and self-development. I never cease to be amazed and motivated by the responses. Some have learned to swim, started their own business, returned to school after 15 or 20 years' absence, changed careers, and many conquered a particular fear. My young-at-heart mother (now 78 and a very active community volunteer) learned to swim at age 65. She swims regularly four times a week and is so proud of having overcome her fear of deep water. I have personally worked on conquering fears — public speaking, flying in small aircraft, skiing, to name just a few. One statement motivated me to rid myself of foolish fears: "Do the things you fear to do and the fear goes away." How true! Challenge yourself... risk with a purpose... and set your goals higher.

"Don't go to your grave with the music still in you!"

On...Selling Yourself Successfully

One of the prerequisites I have set for my daughters Diane and Karen prior to university attendance is to take a 4-day professional sales course with my good friend and colleague, Paul MacDonald. It's not that Diane and Karen have decided to enter the sales profession, but rather I believe it's critical that they acquire an understanding of the psychology of selling. We are all selling in today's competitive marketplace — we sell ourselves, our ideas, our service. As a mother, teacher, coach, and sales manager I was constantly "selling." I continue to do so in my role as a speaker and performance consultant.

It is important for career enhancement and personal satisfaction to devise creative and innovative ways to develop a strong image and impact when communicating to others. People like to do business with a winner — someone with a strong sense of purpose, a positive self-image and an enthusiastic approach to living. We can all develop the creative edge by changing attitudes and behavior.

The following suggestions have worked well for me:

1. Greet everyone you meet with a few positive words and a firm, confident handshake. Communicate a strong sense of yourself to others.

2. Call people by name. Use their name in conversing or in the middle of a letter. Work at remembering people's names and personalize all forms of communication.

3. Go the EXTRA MILE by giving more than the other person expects. It is said that the secret of living is in giving and we should always strive to be "others-centered."

4. Always use a personal and/or business card for a more professional impact. It also helps the receiver in remembering you, the spelling of your name and the nature of your business.

5. Send a note, card, letter, interesting article, or reprint to a friend, customer, or relative expressing a positive quotation, philosophy or word of encourage-

ment. I feel good when I help others feel good about themselves. And *how you feel is everything!*

6. Join a service or business organization unrelated to your occupation. The experience offers an opportunity for growth, networking, experiencing team building, serving on committees — even the possibility of holding executive office. All of these will enhance that future résumé outlining your personal leadership qualities.

7. Have your "colors" done for greater personal impact and increased self-confidence, and include a copy of John Molloy's book *Dress for Success* in your personal development library.

8. Take a public speaking course at a community college or join a speaker's association. Since communication is such a vital skill, any improvement in your verbal and nonverbal techniques will strongly enhance your personal leadership skills.

I tuned in on a TV program recently and heard a professor saying that, in polling 1,000 professional people, 70% said they have received little or no training in interpersonal skills. If you have a choice between being book smart or people smart, be people smart!

9. In an attempt to read, plan, and implement all of these growthful ideas, you may have to join the Six O'clock Club to create more time. Simply set your alarm one hour earlier each day and you'll have the time needed to read, plan, create, and exercise your way to even greater personal satisfaction.

In creating better interpersonal relationships and

more positive results from both a personal and professional point, try to implement the concepts outlined. Winners use these and many other techniques in an attempt to "work smarter, not harder." People gain a positive or negative impression of you during the first four minutes of being introduced. Make those four minutes work to your advantage!

"Your Success Is Your Business!"

On...Motivation — Potential and You!

Studies of successful people show that a mere 15 percent of their success is due to technical training while a whopping 85 percent is attributable to personality development. There are two "games" to work on: The outer game (training) and the inner game (development). Working at developing the latter game involves setting intangible goals to achieve growth through change of attitude and behavior.

As a performance consultant, I encourage people to develop their personal leadership skills in the areas of:

- Time Management
- Communications
- Team Building
- Personal Motivation
- Positive Attitude
- Goals/Plans

A teacher in one of my seminars commented, "The

educational system teaches you how to make a living but it doesn't teach you how to live." That you must do for yourself.

Behavioral scientists state that the average person uses a maximum of only 10% of his or her potential. Many insist it's much lower. We have tremendous untapped potential within us — that is, the power or energy we need to develop and achieve our personal goals. All we have to do is use our imagination — visualize our dreams — and with determination, take positive action.

Last year I read, "If you haven't experienced failures — you haven't had success." People who achieve successes are usually those who have had a lot of failures, but they learned from their mistakes. Four years ago, I experienced a major financial setback due to a business investment loss. Recalling the quotation, "Winners never quit and quitters never win," I wrote a new plan of action and got right back on the winning track.

In my talks, I use the analogy, "The mind is like a parachute; it functions only when it's open." Be open to new concepts and take calculated risks to get ahead. You can always better your best, but you must go out on a limb to get the fruit. "Risking with a purpose is the key to success." My first mentor, my father, gave me a business tip the other day when I asked his advice regarding business expansion. "Speculate to accumulate," he replied. We all should invest in ourselves — any money you spend on developing your potential pays life-long dividends.

Every month I write on my calendar **YASNY** —
You **A**in't **S**een **N**othin' **Y**et! I know and understand
the untapped inner resource of human potential. As
Denis Waitley writes: "Winners see risk as an oppor-
tunity. They see the rewards of success in advance.
They do not fear the penalties of failure."

Because so many of us are visual learners, I use
various visuals in my presentations — one being the
dyna swing (pictured in the photo at the beginning of
this chapter). It represents Newton's third law of
motion — "for every action exerted, there is equal and
opposite reaction." Or, what you give out in life is
what you get back.

We are told that the secret of living is in giving.
Work daily at being "other centered" (BOSA-1). Give
more in your work, service, product, or presentation
than is expected. When you give people excellent
service an automatic referral network begins on your
behalf. All of my speaking engagements to date are by
referral or repeat booking. We keep on following the
"win-win" technique and our business continues to
grow.

As Walt Disney writes: "Do whatever you do so
well, people will want to see you do it again, and they
will bring other people to see what you do so well."

As you work on developing your creative edge,
remember the success formula:

PMA + GOALS = SUCCESS

I would strongly challenge you to write down on a
3 x 5 card or in your planner the two best ideas from
this chapter, *what* they are and *how* you intend to put

these ideas into play — action.

One of my favorite speakers, James Rohn, tells us that the job never gets easier, we get better... so work harder on yourself than you do on the job.

Develop your creative edge, use imagination, stretch yourself by risking more, and start NOW by writing a personal and business game plan for the coming year.

Remember — winners have purpose and a game plan; they keep score daily, and they continually strive for success — by achieving their personal goals.

"If it is to be, it is up to me!"

On...Creativity

"The person who follows the crowd, will usually get no further than the crowd. The person who walks alone is likely to find himself in places no one has ever been before.

Creativity in living is not without its attendant difficulties, for peculiarity breeds contempt. And the unfortunate thing about being ahead of your time is that when people finally realize you were right, they'll say it was obvious all along.

You have two choices in life: You can dissolve into the mainstream, or you can be distinct. To be distinct, you must be different. To be different, you must strive to be what no one else but you can be..."

- Author unknown

Gerald Olivero, Ph.D.
Human Resource Solutions, Inc.
200 Park Avenue, Suite 303E
New York, NY 10166-0105
(212) 316-2800

Gerald Olivero, Ph.D.
As a New York State Licensed Industrial Psychologist, Dr. Olivero has consulted to many distinguished corporations across numerous industries regarding the enhancement of departmental or company-wide productivity and satisfaction. As a speaker and trainer, he has inspired American, British, Canadian, and Singaporean audiences to improve managerial skills, team collaboration, and individual growth.

Dr. Olivero is President of Human Resource Solutions (HRS) which provides organization development consultations and individual career counseling. Prior to founding HRS, he was Vice President, Human Resource Development at PA Consulting; Manager, Organization Development at RCA; Senior Consultant at Merrill Lynch; and Senior Analyst at Prudential.

Dr. Olivero received his B.A. in Psychology from U.C.L.A., his M.A. and Ph.D. in Industrial and Organizational Psychology from The Ohio State University, and worked in Communications Intelligence while in the U.S. Air Force.

His affiliations include: the American Psychological Association; the American Society for Training and Development; the New York Organization Development Network; and the Metropolitan New York Association for Applied Psychology, where he served as President. He is a Reviewer for the Journal of Applied Psychology *and is referenced in* Who's Who in America.

Your Mind and Success

By Gerald Olivero, Ph.D.

*"There is nothing capricious in nature,
and the implanting of a desire indicates
that its gratification is in the constitution
of the creature that feels it."*
                                        - Ralph Waldo Emerson

Although I agree with Webster's dictionary definition of success ("the attainment of wealth, favor, or eminence"), I feel that too much that is important is left unsaid. Consequently, my definition incorporates numerous "success elements" which derive from my experience and writings by authors like Napoleon

Hill, Paul Meyer, Earl Nightingale, Clement Stone,
and Denis Waitley:

- FEELING GOOD, having HIGH SELF-ES-
  TEEM, and a sense of SELF-WORTH.
- Being HAPPY with yourself, even though you
  want to make changes.
- Being GLAD TO BE ALIVE.
- Enjoying GOOD HEALTH in body, mind and
  spirit.
- LOVING YOURSELF and others as well as
  being LOVED BY OTHERS.
- Being ABLE to PROGRESSIVELY REALIZE
  your worthwhile GOALS.
- ATTRACTING those people with whom you
  want to share experiences.
- WINNING, or attaining your desired standing,
  in competition.
- MONETARILY AFFORDING the way of life
  YOU CHOOSE.
- Having the power to REMEMBER INFORMA-
  TION and SOLVE YOUR PROBLEMS.

Considering all of the above elements, success is a
happy way of life, not an end state. I conceive of a
journey, not a destination. Specifying elements of
success enables us to incorporate into our lives those
which would make us happy at any point in time. It
also enables us to define success uniquely for ourselves. Following several principles helps to incorporate success elements into our lives. What are these
principles?

The First Principle:
USE MORE of your MIND'S CAPACITY.

A review of some facts will convince us that we *can* use more of our mind's capacity. Writings by Herbert Benson or Marc Jeannerod make it clear that our mind's capacity is immense. Our bodies contain a nervous system (including the brain) for our use. This system controls our actions and is comprised of over 100 billion nerve cells (neurons), spaces between neuron endings (synapses), and chemicals enabling neurons to "connect" across the synapses (neurotransmitters). Sensations, thoughts and feelings are encoded in specific patterns of neuronal connections (engrams) to form our memory. There are at least 25 nonillion connections — many trillions more than would be required to control our actions or learn a lifetime's worth of information.

Brain Waves

The Diagram Group (collaborating neurologists, physicians, psychologists, editors, and artists), reports that the brain constantly has waves of electrical energy pulsing through it. Certain pulse speeds predominate during various stages of consciousness. Beta waves, about 14-30 cycles per second (cps), predominate during our alert state. Alpha waves (about 8-13 cps) predominate when we relax with eyes closed. Theta waves (about 4-7 cps) predominate during frustration. Delta waves (about 0.5-3 cps) predominate during sleep. Andrew Neher cites evidence that creative innovators such as Albert Einstein and Thomas Edison had many of their insights while they relaxed and used imagery (mental pictures or scenarios).

Left and Right Brains

Michael Gazzaniga, J. LeDoux, Roger Sperry and others document that the left and right hemispheres of our brain tend to have distinctive functions. Silvano Arieti concludes that imagery integrates left and right-brain functions. Therefore, knowledge contained in our logical, rational, language-oriented left-brain can integrate with the knowledge contained in the intuitive, creative, spatially-oriented right-brain. The above left and right-brain split applies to right-handed people. In the case of left-handed individuals, the functions and orientations of the brain hemispheres are reversed.

Conscious and Subconscious Minds

Common evidence for the existence of the subconscious mind is that we have all experienced hunches, insights, intuitions and extra sensory perceptions.

Taken all together, the above is commonly called our "sixth sense." Any thought or sensation that reaches our mind through any of our senses is classified and recorded. If we are aware of the information, it is conscious; if we are not aware, it is subconscious. Sigmund Freud has shown that the subconscious mind has a tremendous influence over what we do and experience, whether or not we are aware of it.

It is often said that people tend to use only about 15% of their mind's capacity — why? My hypothesis (derived from my experience and writings by Freud, Charles Turner and John Randall) is that the nervous system functions at both the "conscious" and "subconscious" levels. Further, most people don't know how to access that part of the mind which contains most of our mind's capacity — the subconscious.

Benson and others report that researchers have not been able to locate our minds. Notwithstanding that researchers have associated the limbic and hypothalamic brain systems with feelings; it is also true that we feel sadness in our hearts, fear in our stomachs, exhilaration in our spinal cords, and know when someone is standing behind us. These facts lead me to conclude that we should consider more than the brain alone when trying to locate the mind. My hypothesis (assuming right handedness) is that the location of the conscious mind is all engrams in the left-brain, while the location of the subconscious mind is all engrams in the right-brain *plus* all other engrams throughout our nervous system.

Much of the information that is in our subconscious is negative and restrictive. It got there during the unduly harsh birth process that most of us experienced and while we were growing up. Remember how our well intentioned parents, family, and friends told us countless times, "No," "Don't," "Can't" and persuaded us that we could not do what we wanted to do? Since the mind influences us to act on the dominant information and thoughts it contains, it is fortunate that we can voluntarily plant any positive thoughts we wish in order to overcome the negative information which the subconscious already contains.

Reprogramming the Mind

How do we tap into the subconscious and reprogram it (add engrams) with the positive information we need in order to more readily attain success? One way is to use subliminal stimuli, however, my preference is to use personalized perceptible stimuli as explained below. Learning to RELAX AT THE ALPHA LEVEL is the key because that state of consciousness facilitates the movement of information from the conscious to the subconscious mind as well as the reverse. With the appropriate information in both conscious and subconscious minds, you will then be more able to REMEMBER INFORMATION and, therefore, increase your PROBLEM SOLVING competence.

Prerecord Affirmations

Before relaxing, record on audio tape 20 minutes of affirmations. Your messages should be personalized and stated positively AS IF THEY WERE ALREADY TRUE. For example:
- "I can lose weight."
- "I am an excellent salesperson."
- "I have $750,000 in cash."
- "I am at peace with myself and others," etc.

Relax at Alpha Level

To attain the relaxed alpha state and ACCESS THE SUBCONSCIOUS MIND:
- Find a quiet spot (no interruptions for 20 minutes).
- Sit or lie down quietly.
- Close your eyes.
- Relax your muscles.
- In rhythm with your breathing, silently repeat any word or phrase which is comforting to you. For example, "One," "Peace," "Love," "Light," "Long Life," "Heavenly Father," etc.

Eastern meditation techniques such as Transcendental Meditation teach us to use sound patterns (mantras) like, "Shr-rem," "Shr-rang," or "Aumm." The purpose of silently repeating a word, phrase or mantra is to clear your mind of all other thought during the relaxation period (meditation). When an extraneous thought does enter your mind during meditation, don't worry about or dwell on it, just resume your repetitive mantra. You will be in the relaxed Alpha state within 20 minutes. Utlilizing biofeedback techniques or hypnosis can also yield the same Alpha state of consciousness. A more recent name for this relaxed state was coined by Benson: the "relaxation response." You will FEEL GOOD during and after meditation.

Listen to Affirmations

Since our subconscious mind is most receptive when relaxed, the time for reprogramming with affirmations is immediately after attaining the Alpha state. Without disturbing your relaxation (don't get up or move around quickly), listen to your prerecorded affirmations with your eyes closed. Reading affirmations may not work because, according to The Diagram Group, 1/3 of their sample lost the Alpha state when their eyes were opened. Experiment, find out if listening or reading is best for you.

Repetition of affirmations is fine. Your subconscious mind accepts all information as fact. Consider that you think your dreams are fact when you are dreaming. Consequently, repeating affirmations will provide your subconscious mind with more information to accept AS FACT.

Affirmations will also help you to have HIGHER

SELF-ESTEEM and a sense of SELF-WORTH. Finally, affirmations help build the FAITH you need to feel CONFIDENT.

Imagination

Your conscious mind will then devise ways of bringing your affirmations to reality. Your imagination is a faculty of your conscious mind. It provides shape, form, and action possibilities to your desires. You can create or attain anything your mind can imagine. When limitations are encountered your imagination comes up with solutions. Overall, what I am saying is: LEARN HOW TO ACCESS YOUR SUBCONSCIOUS MIND SO THAT MORE OF YOUR TOTAL MIND WILL WORK FOR YOU.

The Second Principle:
DECIDE what you want, then GET IT.

If you are not sure what you really want, then begin by getting your life priorities straight. Many successful people (presidents, inventors, business giants, etc.) share the same rank ordering of life priorities, they:

- Develop their mind, body, and spirit.
- Build and love a family.
- Pursue their careers with great intensity.

Pursue only those things that you really want. Don't waste time and energy on what you don't really want. You will not have enough time to pursue everything. Therefore, decide what to pursue, then with confident thought and disciplined action — get it. In relation to thought, remember Nightingale's strangest secret, "You and I become what we think about most." To his secret I would add, "...either consciously or subconsciously." In relation to action, consider the following:

Getting It

Once you've decided what you want, for example, financial independence, you'll need to set goals, make plans to attain the goals, and act on your plans. The process of actively setting and pursuing goals oftentimes makes people feel GLAD TO BE ALIVE. The writings of Hill, Meyer, Waitley and my own experiences have taught me that there are several things involved in order for goal setting, planning and action to yield the desired outcome. What is involved?

lst there is SPECIFICITY. Determine exactly how much money you want — you need to be precise.

2nd there is GIVING. Determine exactly what you will give up for the money — don't expect something for nothing. You may need to ACQUIRE SPECIALIZED KNOWLEDGE of the service or product you intend to give in return for the money. Give yourself the *knowledge to win* over your competitors.

3rd there is PLANNING. Devise a written, detailed plan for how you will get that money. Meyer reports that the single most discriminating factor between achievers and non-achievers is that achievers always have WRITTEN PLANS for what they are going to do.

4th there is TIME. As part of your plan, establish a definite date by which you will have all the money. The date you set must take into consideration the time it will take to give your service or product in return for the money. You must also learn to MANAGE TIME and OVERCOME PROCRASTINATION. You can manage time by *sticking to the time frames of your plans, eliminating time wasters, and delegating to others.* You can overcome procrastination by *reaching timely decisions.* Meyer points out that the lack of timely decision making is a major cause of failure.

5th there is DISCIPLINED ACTION. After planning, begin at once to act in a focused, orderly manner on your plan. Don't wait until all conditions are perfect, they seldom are. Taking disciplined action will convince you that you can PROGRESSIVELY REALIZE YOUR GOALS.

6th there is PERSISTENCE. Persistence is often the key difference between success and failure. Once you've specified your goal — stay with it. Eliminate from your sphere of influence those who will sway you from your goals by practicing ridicule and cynicism. You don't necessarily need to drop the cynics from your circle of friends completely, but you may need to spend more time with supporters. In this manner you can CHOOSE to live life the way you want to live it.

The above procedure works for attaining money or any goal. Prior to using the above procedure, I found that fear, inhibition and doubt frequently dominated my thinking. I also found it easier to engage in disciplined action when I knew why and when I was supposed to do something. Naturally, the above procedure also requires the expenditure of effort, leading us to the next principle:

The Third Principle:
KEEP PHYSICALLY FIT.

- Eat nutritious foods.
- Eliminate substance abuses.
- Get sufficient rest.
- Exercise regularly.
- Practice relaxation.

Physical fitness helps us to cope with life's inevitable stressors and to generate enough energy to do all the *work required* for success. Understand that there is a definite relationship between the body and the mind. A HEALTHY body enables us to have a CONFIDENT mind.

The Fourth Principal:
MAXIMIZE YOUR ATTRACTIVENESS.

In order to attain your goals, you will oftentimes need the help of other people. Research shows that people tend to be drawn towards those who are physically attractive. Therefore:
- Practice good hygiene.
- Maintain your preferred body weight.
- Dress appropriately.

Dressing appropriately does not have to involve expensive, fancy attire. Just ensure that your business outfits are conservative, color coordinated, and properly fitted. Other, more important, ways to attract the people you want are:

Be Cheerful and Grateful

Let people be happy to see you because you are cheerful. Also, tell those who have helped you that you are grateful for their help. Realize that everyone wears an invisible sign that they hope you will see — it reads, "MAKE ME FEEL GOOD!"

Satisfy Others' Needs

Another way to attract people is to arrange for them to RECEIVE BENEFITS from associating with you.

Choose associates who share your goals and support your efforts. However, regardless who you choose, no one will associate with you for a long time without some sort of compensation. The compensation doesn't necessarily have to be monetary, but it should satisfy their needs. Ask what you can do for them, then do it.

If your goal requires interdependent tasks to be performed by a number of people, then these people may be conceived of as a "work team." Special needs are created when you are relying on a work team, they are:
- Joint goal setting and collaborative planning.
- Two-way communications between all members.
- Clearly defined roles for each team member.
- Controlling work which has been delegated.
- Decision making and problem solving procedures.
- Actually meeting with your team in one location.

Build Your Team

Maintain perfect harmony between yourself and every member of your team. Engage in "team building." That involves:
- Examining how the team functions.
- Devising plans to improve team functioning.
- Implementing, then evaluating the improvements.

Behave Ethically

Still another way to attract people is to engage in only those transactions which are honest and truly beneficial to all parties. As a result, others will serve you because they know that you serve them without taking advantage of them.

The Fifth Principle:
BE CONFIDENT that you WILL SUCCEED.

It's easy to be enthusiastically confident about positive information. Therefore, THINK POSITIVELY. According to Norman Vincent Peale and others, our thoughts are generally expressed in language; therefore, after meditation, concentrate on a positive personal vocabulary:
- Replace "I will try to ..." with "I will do ..."
- Replace "I have to ..." with "I want to ..."
- Replace "I can't ..." with "I can ...", etc.

Hill and Stone point out that positive thinking gives people the resolve to keep trying after the inevitable setbacks. Realize that the real winners in life experience *more* failures than other people do because they try more often.

Another thing that has helped me to think positively was to drop a bad habit — the habit of telling other people my problems. Explaining your problems

reinforces that negative information in your mind. From the point of view of being happy, it's not what happens to you that matters, it's how you take it that matters. Finally, my paraphrase of the quote that begins this chapter is that we would not have desires unless we were capable of attaining them, so we might as well be confident that we can attain them. We attain what we actively expect to attain. Your expectation is in your mind. Expect to win and you will win more often; expect to lose and you will lose. According to Waitley, expecting to succeed is the most readily identifiable attitudinal characteristic of winners. Attitudes predispose our behaviors. Fortunately, attitudes can be learned. To the "desire to attain" we can add the attitudinal "expectation of attaining." Here's a way:
- Relax at the Alpha level.
- Visualize what you have to do in order to win.
- Visualize yourself having already won.

The attitudinal expectation of winning is strengthened by using either controlled manipulation of imagery (visualization) or affirmations. With visualization, you are adding new, internally generated engrams to your memory. With affirmations, you are also adding new engrams to your memory by listening to or reading from an external source. Researchers like Arieti, Robert Gagne, Richard White, and Graham Wallas, have shown that visualization enhances divergent thought, problem solving, and creativity. Additionally, we have all seen Olympic athletes visualize their routines before the actual physical performance of the routines.

The Sixth Principle:
Nourish your SPIRIT.

Just as researchers have been unable to locate the mind, they have also been unable to locate the spirit. Nevertheless, my hypothesis is that our spirit (life force) is located throughout our bodies in the form of radiant energy, and also extends beyond our body in the same form. The energy which extends beyond our body is our aura.

Another way of putting it is that part of our being is in the form of energy and another part is in the form of mass. The Alpha state increases our receptivity to energy from others or nature. Even if you do not engage in religious practices, you can nourish your spirit. Enhancing your mind and body, and communing with others and nature, especially in the Alpha state, will nourish your spirit.

The more life force energy you have, the better. From it you are internally motivated (have a tendency to exert effort) toward a particular performance level. Research works, including my own, have shown that whether you are motivated to exert effort toward poor performance and negative outcomes (fears) or toward good performance and positive outcomes (desires) is primarily determined by your expectation that your effort will yield the required performance level. You can increase your expectation that your maximum effort will yield good performance and positive outcomes by using affirmations and visualization.

You *can* give yourself the mental, physical, and spiritual strength you need to PROGRESSIVELY SUCCEED in goal attainment and BE HAPPY.

BIBLIOGRAPHY

S. Arieti. *Creativity: The Magic Synthesis.* New York: Basic Books, 1976.

H. Benson. *Your Maximum Mind.* New York: Random House, 1987.

The Diagram Group. *The Brain: A User's Manual.* New York: Perigee Books, 1987.

R.M. Gagne. *The Conditions of Learning.* New York: Holt, Rinehart & Winston, 1977.

R.M. Gagne and R.T. White. "Memory Structures and Learning Outcomes," *Review of Educational Research.* Vol. 48, pp. 187-222, 1978.

M.S. Gazzaniga and J. LeDoux. *The Integrated Mind.* New York: Plenum, 1978.

N. Hill and W.C. Stone. *Success Through a Positive Mental Attitude.* (cassettes), Chicago, Illinois: Nightingale - Conant Corporation, 1988.

M. Jeannerod. *The Brain Machine: The Development of Neurological Thought.* Cambridge Massachusetts: Harvard University Press, 1985.

P.J. Meyer. *Dynamics of Personal Goal Setting & Time Control.* Waco, Texas: Success Motivation International, 1984.

A. Neher. *The Psychology of Transcendence.* Englewood Cliffs, New Jersey: Prentice-Hall, 1980.

E. Nightingale (Narrator). Condensation of N. Hill's *Think and Grow Rich* . (cassette), Waco, Texas: Success Motivation International, 1960.

G. Olivero, *Expectancy Theory Predictions of Motivation Moderated by Race, Sex and Socioeconomic Status.* Doctoral Dissertation, Columbus, Ohio: The Ohio State University; pp. 99, 120, 122; 1973.

N.V. Peale. *The Power of Positive Thinking.* Greenwich, Connecticut: Fawcett Crest, 1956.

J.H. Randall. *The Making of the Modern Mind.* Boston: Houghton Mifflin, 1940.

R.W. Sperry. "Cerebral Organization and Behavior", *Science.* Vol.133, pp. 1749-1757, 1961.

C.H. Turner. *Maps of the Mind.* New York: Macmillan, 1981.

Webster.s New Collegiate Dictionary. Springfield, Massachusetts: Merriam, 1974.

D.E. Waitley. *The Psychology of Winning.* (cassettes), Chicago, Illinois: Nightingdale - Conant Corporation, 1978.

G. Wallas. *The Art of Thought.* New York: Harcourt & Brace, 1926.

Lana Bates
Bates Marketing Services
1929 White Oak
Wichita, KS 67207
(316) 683-5316

Lana Bates

Lana Bates is a well known authority on building businesses and developing personal growth. As a consultant and dynamic speaker she can take a complex subject and almost miraculously turn it into action and results.

She has spoken to hundreds of people on diverse subjects, to companies like Prudential Bache, Vocational Association, Xerox Americare and The American Diabetes Association.

As President of Bates Marketing Services she is a consultant on innovation, specializing in company growth and new ventures. She is also founder of the Pathways Institute: a Center for Personal and Business Development.

In the past she has owned and operated five successful businesses. She has traveled extensively in the U.S. and Europe, speaks fluent French and is an avid reader with a large library. This wealth of knowledge and experience has enabled her to become a master story teller who can hold the interest of an audience with examples, humor and concrete ideas.

She has authored many articles, newsletters and a soon-to-be published personal development book.

Acknowledged as a talented and creative individual, she was chosen as runner-up to Mrs. Kansas in 1984. Her recognized expertise in business and marketing has also won her a national design award as well as the Woman of the Year Achievement Award.

Seven Surefire Steps to Selling Your Creative Ideas

By Lana Bates

"The man with a new idea is a crank —
until the idea succeeds."
                    - Mark Twain

As I looked at my newborn son for the first time, a rosy squalling miniature person, I thought to myself, "Could there be anything more perfect than this?" I was to find out later that things can sometimes be a little less than perfect. Babies, I found out, were a great deal of work. Often they cried. They always needed food. And besides that, they didn't sleep all night! Now, however, years later, I am beginning to see the fruits of all that hard work. A pleasant, more self-sufficient, responsible human being has emerged, giving me a great deal of satisfaction.

The creation of a new idea is like the birth of a child. The idea seems so perfect in the beginning. As you work with the idea you begin to realize there are obstacles that have to be overcome and that it is only after a lot of hard work that you begin to see it develop. It is only then that the great plans you envisioned begin to take place.

Sometimes we are creative simply for our own satisfaction, like an artist producing a painting for himself that is not for sale. However, most of our creative efforts are for gain or for promoting it in some other way. That is what this chapter is all about — selling our creative ideas for profit, or to persuade someone to our way of thinking.

The special techniques given in this chapter can apply to selling anything, but they are especially needed when we are dealing with something new or innovative. We need to understand that people resist change and that possible prospects will remain uncommitted to an idea unless it is pointed out in graphic form the benefits of changing their ways. It's human nature — not to be resented — merely understood. Therefore an organized step-by-step plan is needed.

By the way, if you feel guilty about trying to

promote your ideas for profit, remember that our world is structured on the philosophy of a fair exchange.

David Ogilvy, the great advertising entrepreneur who founded Ogilvy & Mather, makes no bones about the motivational effect of pursuing money: "Many of the greatest creations of man have been inspired by the desire to make money. When George Frederick Handel was on his beam ends, he shut himself up for twenty-one days and emerged with the complete score of The Messiah — and hit the jackpot. At the end of a concert at Carnegie Hall, Walter Damrosch asked Rachmaninoff what sublime thoughts had passed through his head as he stared out into the audience during the playing of his concerto. 'I was counting the house,' said Rachmaninoff."

The Prerequisites

There are several prerequisites for selling your ideas or persuading others:

Research. Some of us may need to do some research to find out if our idea really is innovative. Has someone else already beat us to the draw? Better to know it now than after a lot of time and effort has been expended.

Belief. We need to have a deep abiding belief in ourselves and in our idea. If *we* don't deeply care about it, then how could we convince someone else that it matters?

Persistence. Persistence is paramount to success. Selling an idea — especially a new idea — is hard work. There will be disappointments along the way. Often people that you expected to support you, don't. Even sometimes those who are very close to you. Persistence in the face of rejection and discouragement is the only way great ideas are ever produced and brought into reality.

Networking. We can mine our contacts not only to get prospects but to find mentors. There are many people in this world who are generous with their time and will help us if we will just ask.

With research, belief, persistence and networking we are ready to move on. It is at this point we begin the seven step process to sell our creative ideas or to persuade others.

1. Objective

Ask: what is the single most important objective in selling this idea? Choose only the most important reason. Is it to earn more money? Perhaps it's to become more well known in your profession. Maybe the idea is so novel that you feel it will help others as well as bring in a profit. Whatever it is, remember to choose only one major goal.

In this objective, we must state exactly what it is we want. It must also be measurable. If it isn't something with tangible or measurable evidence, how will we know when we have accomplished it? Set an exact date when you would like to complete the task. An objective is important because it is impossible to set about planning something when we are not even sure what it is we are working for.

Sometime ago I met a pro-football referee. It was close to the time when the professional football players were going to go on strike. Interestingly enough, he said that he had the instinct that some of their objectives may not have been as clear as they should have been. Their immediate objective for going on strike was to give them more benefits. However, if some football players had known they would eventually lose their jobs, they may have reconsidered. If the major objective was, in fact, to play ball, then striking for more benefits might not have been worth risking the primary objective, which was to stay on the team. Knowing our objective determines the specific actions we will take.

A typical objective might read: "My product will be on store shelves by Christmas of this year"; or, "By June of this year I will convince my boss that I need to take a research sabbatical on our new product line."

2. Target Audience

Define who it is you're trying to persuade, or decide who it is that will buy your product. Be able to visualize in your mind that person, or at least a representative of that group. Know as much about your audience as you possibly can, because it is around that audience that you will devise your plan.

If you write a proposal, give a speech, or produce a brochure that doesn't appeal to your target audience, you have wasted both your money and your energy.

You can't please everyone or address every audience. I used to go to a lot of football games. Sometimes an airplane would fly over during half-time and dump onto the audience thousands of papers — propaganda of some kind or another.

Contrast this with a personal letter sent to my own mail box. The difference between the flyers dropped on the masses of people and the letter, is that the letter was directed specifically to me. This is the kind of targeting we must focus on. We build the message around a specific audience.

3. The Hook

The hook is the grabber. It attracts the person right away. It's the title or benefit that makes him want to hear more.

Let's say you have an idea you'd like the company to adopt. So you walk in and say to your boss, "Would you listen to a new idea if I told you I could increase the total revenues of this company twofold within the next twelve months?" The objective was that you wanted him to accept your idea. You knew who your audience was. You knew exactly what he was going to be interested in, so your opening words were a dramatic hook that immediately got him interested.

When you are trying to think of a hook, select the single most dramatic benefit of your idea. Decide what interests your audience most. Look at your product or idea through their eyes. Spend some time "walking in their moccasins," as the old Indian saying goes. Pretend that you are them, then decide what it would take to convince you to accept this idea or innovative product.

Sometime ago I read an article about the history of our currency. To some people this may seem rather boring. However, I have to admit that the opening sentence grabbed my attention: "THERE ARE TWENTY-SIX STATES PRINTED ON THE BACK OF A FIVE-DOLLAR BILL!"

That statement wasn't boring at all. In fact, it hooked me so well, I not only read the article but got out a magnifying glass and a five-dollar bill to see if it were true. Sure enough, there were the names of the states! This is precisely what we have to do when we talk to someone about our idea. We have to grab their interest immediately.

4. The Plan

When I was a little girl I can remember going often to visit my grandparents. When we had to stay overnight, I would listen for the gracious old grandfather clock to chime, chime, chime all through the night. I was fascinated by it. I wondered how all those parts and gears and pulleys and chimes could all work together so well. I have decided that a well-worked plan is orchestrated in exactly the same way. All the pieces fit together to produce the effect you want: to achieve the objective which you have set for yourself.

There are several approaches to creating a plan. I use the **ABC** approach:

A. Brainstorm by listing all possible tasks that are to be accomplished. Prioritize them and then delegate whenever possible.

B. Schedule all tasks on a calendar including major milestones with their appropriate due dates. That way you know not only WHAT needs to be done but WHEN it needs to be done. Check the calendar daily to be aware of any due dates that are coming up and any immediate tasks that need to be done.

C. Break up big jobs into "bite size" pieces so they are not as overwhelming. Even large projects have small jobs that don't take more than ten or fifteen minutes to do. Be sure to write them down and check them off as you finish them. After all, that is part of the reward of accomplishing a job.

Writing an organized plan and breaking the jobs into more manageable tasks also helps to prevent procrastination, the deadly enemy of creativity.

5. Methods

If an OBJECTIVE is an overview and the PLAN is a strategy, then the METHODS are the specific techniques used to carry out that plan. Typical methods are: documents, such as a résumé, business plan, marketing strategy or proposal.

If you have a product that is meant for a mass audience, then you will use advertising techniques like print ads, TV and radio commercials, billboards and brochures. Trying to persuade a group to your way of thinking would include speeches and presentations. Proposals and memos are often used to communicate new ideas to your boss.

Other methods include systems for follow-up, since much of our credibility is based on doing what we say we'll do. Keeping records of call-backs, leads and data that has been sent, helps us to be competitive and organized.

A great example of using every method possible to accomplish an objective was when McDonald's prepared to open up the hamburger market in Japan. They had a problem. The first store they were going to open was in a shopping mall and the rule was that no one could tie up the area for remodeling for more than 39 hours. However, their objective was clear; set up a unit in Japan. So they mapped out a plan describing specific procedures and techniques. They used every method available to streamline the operation. They practiced the setup of the store four times in a warehouse. The day they put it into the mall, they not only set it up in the 39 hours, but with time to spare.

To sell our ideas for profit we have to use every method possible as long as it meets our objective.

6. Ask

Ask for the order! Ask for action! Ask for a commitment! How many times do we tell our story, give our speech, do the sales pitch and then become nervous about asking for a commitment. We're afraid we'll be turned down. But look at it this way: We have done too much work up to this point not to take this vital step. It is critical. It is the moment of reckoning. Instinctively we know it, yet it's often easier to just not ask.

When my teenage son walks into the room with a certain swagger, I know he is going to ask me for something. I know it before he even starts to speak. I can be sure he has a thoroughly persuasive argument. He will launch into all the various and intricate reasons why he should have a particular sum of money. And when he gets finished, do you think he is going to turn around and walk out the door? Absolutely not! He'll look at me straight in the eye and say, "All right, Mom, all I need is ten dollars." Have you ever known a teenager to come in and tell you *why* he needs the car and then walk out without asking you for it? No! He puts his hand out for the keys. That is the kind of dogged determination we need to have when it comes to selling our ideas.

7. Evaluation

Recently I went to a formal ball, an impressive affair, with women in long gowns and men in tuxedos. After the sumptuous banquet and as the people began to move across the floor dancing to the music of the orchestra, a beautiful, elegant woman entered the hall from the direction of the powder room. Seeing her partner across the room, she made her way gracefully towards him. As her long gown swept across the floor, we soon noticed she was also swishing a long trail of tiolet tissuepaper. It extended all the way across the floor, down the hall and into the powder room. There was a great deal of fluttering and tittering as several of the ladies in the room hurried to her assistance. If this beautiful woman had looked back with a quick glance in the mirror before she left the powder room she would never have headed in the direction of the ballroom. That backward glance could have saved her a great deal of embarrassment.

When we identify an objective and commit to a plan, we are only being fair to ourselves to look back and evaluate where we have been and whether or not we have achieved what we have set out to do.

That evaluation will also point out, sometimes

painfully, what we could have done better, and also helps us determine where we wish to go next.

Putting It All Together

Well there it is! Seven simple but powerful steps to sell your ideas for profit. We select one major OBJEC-TIVE so we know exactly *where* we are going. We need to know *who* we are going to talk to; that's our TARGET AUDIENCE. Then we HOOK them immediately with a *benefit* that interests them. We set up a PLAN and organize the *system* that will help us to carry out our objective. We identify the specific METHODS needed to *carry out* that plan. When we are face to face with our prospect we ASK for the order, the *commitment*. And finally, we *look back*, EVALUATE the process and reward ourselves for what we have accomplished.

Some years ago I had the opportunity to go to a survival camp. You know the kind, where you're dropped off in the middle of desolation and you have to learn how to survive on the land, spend the nights by yourself, start your own fires, procure you own food and participate in life skills and group activities.

On one of the days as we were taking a treacherous hike, we reached what we felt with relief was the end of our trek. We discovered as we approached the area that it was a high cliff. We were on top. Where we needed to go was at the bottom. We had to learn how to rappel over the side of the cliff! There was no turning back or the course would not be considered complete. It was obvious there were risks involved. Would the rope hold? What would happen if we made a mistake and couldn't hold on properly? With no other choice, we choked back all thoughts of risk and each person proceeded to take his turn. When it was time for me, they tied the rope around my waist. I'll never forget the moment when I stood on the edge of the cliff. It was my turn and I was determined to do it. As is typical in a situation like this, time slowed as I leaned forward into midair. I pulled myself over the edge of the cliff and looked straight down. I was face forward, which is considered commando style. Yes, I was scared. Surprisingly, however, I was also exhilarated. I strode down the side of the cliff forgetting all my frightened feelings and the danger. I concentrated on what I was supposed to be doing. Someone later told me that by the time I reached the bottom I was singing at the top of my voice. Amazing what a little adrenaline will do!

Selling a creative idea or persuading others is a lot like rappelling. Sometimes you reach the point of no return. There is no way you can backtrack. You can only go forward. The rope holding you is the plan you have made. You are dependent on that to carry you down and to hold you securely. Sure, it's frightening, but it's also very exciting when you reach your objective.

That's what risk is all about. There was risk in

going over the cliff. There is also risk any time you try to convince someone of your idea or to sell your product. But risk and reward can be balanced. If the reward equals the risk, definitely take the risk!

It's a wonderful experience to be creative, but it is something else entirely to see your idea become reality, to perhaps even *change people's lives.*

"Everyone has talent.
What is rare is the courage to follow the talent
to the places where it leads."
- Erica Jong

Gary Hickingbotham
Mindpower International Pty Ltd.
38 Leonard St.,Upwey,
Vic.3146, Australia
(03) 754 4128 (03) 20 1301

Gary Hickingbotham

Gary is Managing Director of Mindpower International Pty Ltd., a company which specializes in goal setting, sales training, motivation, communication, management and personal development. His company is an authorized distributor for the internationally known Success Motivation Institute (S.M.I.)

Gary has a degree in science and spent sixteen years in the corporate world leading to his appointment as Chief Executive of a manufacturing company. In 1984, he decided to start his own business and has been able to implement his own practical experiences into his informative approach to people development.

In 1986 and 1987, Gary was the leading Australian distributor for S.M.I.

As a member of Jaycees, Gary has devoted many hours in helping other people and working in the community. In 1987 he was awarded the title of Outstanding Jaycee of Australia and then at the World Congress of Jaycees in Amsterdam, Holland of that year, was awarded the Outstanding Jaycee of the World. This award was given to Gary for his involvement and contribution to the Jaycee organization and his tireless work in the community, particularly in showing others how to improve their self leadership skills.

He is a graduate of the Australian Administrative Staff College and a member of the National Speakers Association of Australia.

Gary is married to Janice and has two children, Glenn and Michelle.

Creative Leadership

By Gary R. Hickingbotham

"To be what we are, and to become what we are capable of becoming is the only end in life"
- Robert Louis Stevenson

Like most young people I had wonderful and exciting dreams of the future. I had visions of being a super achiever in business, living in a big house and of being recognized as a world winner, probably in sport.

Up until now I have achieved many goals in my life providing me with a great career, home and lifestyle. Most of all a happy family life with a wonderful wife and two incredibly positive and caring teenage children.

I have not achieved world recognition in sport. But I did become a world award winner in 1987. For it was then in November that I was awarded the title of "Outstanding Jaycee of the World." The Jaycees are an international organization of men and women whose primary purpose is to develop people so they can help make the world a better place in which to live

When this award was announced I found it hard to believe. "Me? A world winner at 38 years of age?"

Friends and associates asked me questions such as, "Gary that's fantastic! How did you do it?" "What can you share with me to help me achieve better results in my life?"

Since receiving my award I've taken time to ask a few questions of myself, review my progress and analyse what it took to achieve such success. I've searched for the ideas I could share with other people to help them achieve better results in their lives.

Personal Leadership

I am convinced one of the keys is self leadership. It's how you take charge of your progress through life. This quality of personal leadership can be defined as:

"The self confident ability to crystallize your thinking so that you are able to establish an exact direction for your own life, to commit yourself to moving in that direction and then to take determined action to acquire, accomplish, or become whatever that goal demands." - P.J. Meyer

In other words, knowing where you want to go in all facets of your life and deciding how you will get there. I have found that when I decide I want something I must ask myself the question, "What do I need to do to lead myself to this particular goal?"

This point really struck me when I changed my career direction several years ago. For sixteen years I worked for other people in the corporate area progressing to my appointment as Chief Executive of a manufacturing company.

I thought this meant security and freedom but I had a vague feeling I was not using enough of my potential. I wanted to start my own business, to break away and see if I could do it. But I had a mortgage to pay, a family to provide for, cars to run, and needed regular money to live. After I thought about this dilemma — which way do I go, do I stay doing what I know, do I continue doing what I was trained to do? Would I make it in my own business? Would my family and lifestyle suffer? Then a quotation from the Bible, Proverbs 23:7, changed my thinking; "As a man thinketh in his heart so is he."

Then I knew I created my own destiny. I knew my thoughts controlled me. I knew that, "if it was to be, it was up to me." I decided that only I could take the step to change my career and once I did that, I was on my own. No one else was there to help me, to guide me, to give me regular monthly salary cheques — it was up to me.

I had to exercise personal leadership in my life. I had no alternative but to lead myself. I had to be creative in planning my life. I had to be innovative.

How often are you faced with a similar decision in your life? It may be a career change, a change in your physical or mental development, a decision in your family life area or a decision that relates to your spiritual growth.

The answer is found when you take control of your life by exercising personal leadership and *leading* your life to a correct decision.

I believe that to initiate, to innovate and create a more successful future for yourself, you need to develop and follow a leadership plan for your life.

The leadership plan that I have followed and recommend to others is one written by Paul J. Meyer, the founder and chairman of the internationally famous Success Motivation Institute.

This simple five step plan is:

Step 1. Crystallize your thinking.

Step 2. Develop a written plan and deadline for the achievement of your goal.

Step 3. Develop a burning desire for the things that you want.

Step 4. Develop a supreme self-confidence in your abilities.

Step 5. Develop unshakable determination to follow through on your plan regardless of circum-stances, criticism or what others say, think or do.

Importance of Vision in Life

In my profession now as a trainer and speaker, many people raise problems like, "I want more from life but I'm not sure if that's for me"; or, "I don't know if that's what I'm meant to do."

In studying successful leaders, whether they are leaders of others or simply effective leaders of their own lives, I have discovered that they all have one thing in common. The common element contained in the great achievements of individuals is what I term the **"Vision Factor."**

Vision is the ability to have a clear picture of what you see happening in your life. If this factor is present in our lives then we must succeed automatically.

Some examples of individuals who had a strong vision are:

• Lee Iacocca - had a vision of turning an almost bankrupt Chrysler into profits and saved hundreds of thousands of jobs.

• Lang Hancock - had a vision of opening up the iron ore mines in the remotest parts of Australia.

• Abraham Lincoln - had a vision of freedom for all citizens that fulfilled the real needs of the people and gave them unity.

• Thomas Edison - had a vision of providing light by harnessing the power of electricity.

• Mother Theresa - has a vision of helping the needy of the world.

What is your vision?

Why is Vision in Life Important?

I have found that by having a vision in every area of life I have become more innovative — I try new things — my creative juices flow and I keep moving forward. I do look for new ways to do things.

Without singular commitment to a vision we cannot lead ourselves in a definite direction. We become a wandering generality rather than a meaningful specific. The factor which separates the mediocre from the great is just this, the vision factor.

Vision provides:
- Direction
- A worthwhile destination
- Motivation
- Enthusiasm
- A sense of achievement

and importantly,
- Fulfillment of our life's purpose.

Purpose is defining the reasons why we are on this planet and for our very being.

One of my purposes in life is to help other people achieve their goals by using more of their potential. My vision is that if I help others I am using my God-given talents to make the world a better place in which to live.

Innovative Leadership Skills

If you want to be better than average then you must do above average things. If you want to be an above average parent then you must do a little more than the average parent does. This may mean spending a few minutes quality time on a daily basis with your children. The average parent spends almost no quality time with their children. Or perhaps it means telling your children *why* you love them. The average parent tells their children that they do love them but forgets the why.

If you want to be an above average business person then you need to do the little things that make the difference. Things such as providing service to clients or paying a little extra attention to the people around you.

An associate of mine believes totally in service and has a motto of, "Promise a lot and deliver more." She sends out thank you notes, recognizes achievements in her clients and cares for others. She is in sales where most salespeople promise a lot and deliver nothing. Her clients are pleasantly surprised when she does provide service. She does above average things and consequently her business is growing rapidly.

Innovative Personal Leadership Skills

Whatever vocation or position you have in life, to experience the thrill of achievement or the feeling that you have used more of your potential you need to develop innovative slight edge skills. Slight edge skills are the little extra things you do in life that put you ahead. These are the skills that unsuccessful people don't attempt or don't want to do. These are thinking and action skills that develop above average results. These are skills that you need to initiate and then implement in your life.

The following are some abilities and skills that will allow you to improve your own personal leadership skills. These are personal leadership skills that will allow you to let life touch you, to allow you to achieve your vision in life and to allow you to say, "this I have done."

1. Goal Setting

Goal setting is the key to accomplishment. Creative goal setting allows us to often achieve goals sooner. Look at different innovative methods. Dare to be different and dare to implement those methods. Most of the major accomplishments of mankind would not have occurred unless creative and innovative goal setting was used.

2. Initiative

We need to exercise initiative in our thinking and apply this in our actions. We need to look at the ways things can be done rather than the ways that they cannot. I'm reminded of a quote from George Bernard Shaw : *"Some men see things as they are and say why? I dream things that never were and say why not?"*

3. Self-Confidence

Creative personal leadership requires that you have confidence in yourself. The only way we gain this self confidence is to expose ourselves to risk. By risking ourselves we gain the experience and the knowledge of how to do a task again and even better.

When I first started in selling I had no confidence in my sales abilities. In fact, after my first sales call I was convinced that I had made a fool of myself and that selling was a profession I should not have ventured into. However, I stuck at it and, as I gained new knowledge I developed experience and my confidence grew. If I had not exposed myself to the possibility of failure then I would have never developed the sales skills I now possess. As Winston Churchill said, "90% of all failure comes from quitting." I could have quit. I would have failed and I would never have gained confidence in selling.

If most failure comes from quitting, then to eliminate most failure in life, *don't quit.*

4. Personal Responsibility

We must take personal responsibility for our own thoughts, actions and feelings. Creative leaders understand this and are in control of their own destiny. If we blame others for our mistakes or claim it's their fault for the way we feel, then we are not in charge of our lives. If we are not in charge, we will never exhibit true personal leadership.

Today it is becoming commonplace in many societies to try and fix the "blame" for a problem or a situation that society finds itself in that is not to its liking. This trend develops dependent people rather than independent ones. *Take charge* of your thoughts, actions and feelings.

5. Healthy Self Image

Self image is our mental picture of the person we think we are. In life there are a number of laws that govern our results. The law of gravity works every time whether we like it or not. Similarly, the self image law works just as surely — *We never rise above the picture we create for ourselves.*

Man cannot exceed his self imposed bonds of limitation.

In May, 1954, part-time English athlete, Roger Bannister, pictured himself breaking the four minute barrier for the mile race. Athletes before him believed that they could not break through this impenetrable barrier. They could not run such a time because their self image picture said it was impossible as nobody else had done it. Bannister did it because he saw himself doing it.

It was only a matter of weeks before the Australian athlete, John Landy, also broke the mythical barrier. Why could he do it? Because somebody else had done it before, and caused his self image to accept that it could be done.

Let your self image run free. Let it be creative. Let it be innovative. Let it transport you to the pinnacles of success.

6. Self Organization

One of the best traits of personal leadership is that of self organization. You must know what to do next for the achievement of your goals.

One of my clients, who is a remarkable achiever, shared the following points in self organization with me when I asked him how he seemed to achieve so much:

• Write everything down - An old Chinese proverb says that the "Shortest pencil is better than the longest memory."

• Use a good diary system - There are many and varied diary systems on the market. My friend tried a different system for six years until he found one that best suited his needs.

• Daily to-do list - Each night before leaving the office my client lists the tasks to be done the following day. Once this is done he arranges them in order of priority. He has discovered that this allows him to have a better night's sleep because his sub-conscious mind knows exactly what he has to do when he wakes up.

• Time management - If you want something done, give it to a busy person. Why? They know how to work on priorities and overcome the insidious habit of procrastination. What my friend does is establish a weekly planner where he allocates specific tasks to specific time blocks in the week. He does exactly what he plans to do. As he has short and long range goals, he finds it easy to decide what to do on a daily basis.

7. P.I.O.S.

P.I.O.S. stands for the "Put it off syndrome." This is simply the tendency for putting tasks off and not taking action on them now.

One of the keys in leading yourself and others is to overcome the P.I.O.S. trap. To do this we need to develop new habits that replace the bad habits.

There are four steps to overcoming P.I.O.S.:

Step 1. Admit that you put things off. To admit this is a commitment to fix it.

Step 2. Learn about procrastination. Understand why you do it. The major reasons that people put things off are:

- insecurity (sub-conscious fears of achievement)
- confusion (undecided what to do next with their life)
- lack of priorities (poor planning)
- forgetfulness (poor memory)
- not accepting personal responsibility
- fear of change (due to indefinite plans, staying in the "comfort zone")
- worry (fear of a future outcome)
- monotony (when they find things boring they can procrastinate)
- psychological fatigue (doing too much - they are not giving their brain sufficient time to rest)

Step 3. Choose a definite plan of action. List the steps you intend to carry out to achieve the desired response.

Step 4. Carry out your plan of action. *Become a "Do it now person."*

8. Study

People who wish to be good at a task need to study. If you want to be a good student you must study. If you want to be a good doctor you study medicine. If you want to be a good accountant you study accountancy. If you want to be a good parent you must study the art of parenting. If you want to be a good leader of yourself and others you must study leadership. This means talking to successful people and asking them how they achieve results. Certainly it also means reading books on leadership and success.

Throughout the history of mankind the remarkable achievers in life have been students. Those who are eager to learn more. Those who want to know how to fine tune themselves.

Innovative Group Leadership Skills

Earlier I discussed the idea that, to be an effective leader of others, you needed to take the first step of leading your life in a positive direction to a definite destination.

Skills and abilities that great leaders of people have are:

1. Attractiveness and Charisma

Great leaders have a certain quality of personal magnetism. There is something about their manner and charisma that others are drawn to. This is an intangible quality but it is a quality we need to work on. What personal characteristics do people find attractive in you? Is it your smile, your caring nature, your positive attitude, your communication ability, your empathy, your wit, your intelligence, your humour, your knowledge or the vision for the future you have? Whatever it is, work on it!

2. Enthusiasm

Enthusiasm for life and the end benefit results of your mission will pull others into the vacuum you create. Enthusiasm literally means "God within," i.e. the power within. Work on the power within you— that ability that can move mountains, take a man to the moon or help a political leader change a nation's complete direction.

I suggest you become enthusiastic about :
- your own very special life
- your career
- your family
- your spiritual beliefs
- your physical goals
- your mental development
- your friends
- the people you may be leading.

3. Communication

The art of communication is an essential tool to influence the thoughts and actions of others. Empathy (knowing and understanding how others feel) is a trademark of effective leadership.

Winston Churchill, Mahatma Gandhi, John F. Kennedy and Abraham Lincoln all had tremendous empathy for the people of their nations. They were in tune with the feelings and thoughts of the people and as a consequence people followed them.

Practice the art of communication and the art of public speaking. Effective leaders understand the power of the spoken word. Take every opportunity to speak to groups — whether they be your employees, associations you may belong to, civic and service clubs, industry associations or your family.

4. Expectancy

Expectancy is letting others know what you expect from them in working towards the group vision. One of the secrets of leadership is to communicate the faith you have in peoples' abilities and have an expectation slightly higher than theirs. In other words, if you expect better results than they think they can contribute, then people will in most cases rise to your expectations.

5. Praise and Recognition

To improve a person's performance, praise and recognition is important for their self esteem.

Let people know you are proud of them and praise

in public. Praising in private is not nearly as effective as praising in public where the individual obtains recognition from of his peers. *Catch people doing things right.*

The Future

To create the future we desire and dream about, we must innovate creative leadership skills.

"If you do what you've always done you'll get what you've always got."

We must change our actions and thoughts if we are not happy with the results we have achieved to date.

Remember,

> *"Leadership is action,*
> *not position."*

Dr. Dorye Roettger
Creative Analyst
3809 De Longpre Ave.
Los Angeles, CA 90027
(213) 665-6444

Dr. Dorye Roettger

Dorye Roettger is a creative analyst, specializing in self-development. She identifies and analyzes problems... finds creative, practical solutions... and designs personal growth systems for both individuals and organizations.

Cited in the Congressional Record (1971) as an "Inspiration to the Nation," she has a strong record of accomplishment in a number of career areas.

A professional musician, Dorye pioneered one of the nation's first nonprofit corporations in the Arts (Festival Players of California) and was a nationally recognized leader for the next 20 years.

She has been a syndicated columnist ("Bridging the Culture Gap"), author, editor and public speaker with stage, radio and television experience. A training director in both the private and public sectors, she has developed and presented many creative educational programs.

Helping others has been the core of Dorye Roettger's professional activity, and the springboard of her extensive research in the arts and the creative process.

Among the many honors and awards she has received are a Toastmasters 1987 Best Speaker Award, a Medal of Honor from the Los Angeles Police Department (where she is a Human Resources consultant), a Coro Foundation Internship, and a California Teaching Credential (she's presently a trainer in the School Volunteer Program of the Los Angeles Unified School District). Dorye has been listed in Who's Who of American Women, The World Who's Who in Music, International Authors and Writers Who's Who, *and others.*

She is also an active participant in the National Speakers Association, International Platform Association, National Writers Club, and American Council for the Arts.

Dorye enjoys a very creative single life with a large "family" of animal companions.

Beyond Performance

By Dr. Dorye Roettger

"There is nothing more difficult...more perilous...or more uncertain in its success than to take the lead in the introduction of a new order of things."
- Jean-Jacques Rousseau

When John Humphrey, co-founder and chairman of The Forum Corporation of North America, accepted an invitation to sit on the Board of Directors of the Boston Ballet Company, he was confident that he would be able to turn the financially ailing group around.

When he started, he has since said, he believed

that he would be successful by bringing effective business tools to the management of ballet.

He did succeed. But more important, he learned a surprising lesson — that is, as a provider of corporate training services, he would be even more successful by bringing ballet tools to the management of business!

For more than twenty-five years, I was a performing artist. Not a ballet dancer, but a concert musician. I was also the founder and executive director of a nonprofit arts organization. And for all of those years, I struggled to achieve financial security, trying to follow the conventional dictate to be more business-like.

And now, here is a man highly respected in the business world coming out and saying that ballet, the most ephemeral of all the arts, might actually have something of value to offer business.

It's an idea that hasn't quite caught on yet. But in these few pages, I'd like to help spread the word.

First of all, what exactly *are* the tools of ballet and other art forms? They are the very tools that you're looking for in this book. The tools of CREATIVITY and INNOVATION. They are the tools that will help you become the kind of human being needed in our rapidly changing world. The kind of person who is prepared for change, able to improvise, face new situations with confidence. The kind of person who can handle the ever-increasing flow of information and meet the challenge of advancing technology. In short, the kind of person who is creative and innovative.

What I want to do is give you a new slant on how to develop these skills.

Creativity in Changing Times

Of course, if you're still not too clear in your mind as to what this creativity talk is really about, don't worry. And don't for a minute think that you're alone. You have, in fact, a lot of company. Very few people, especially those leaders of business and industry who have always prided themselves on their hard, scientific approach to management, feel at all easy with such nebulous concepts as possibility thinking, intuition, mental imagery, and all the rest.

Today, however, those leaders, like you, are facing strange new challenges. The comfortable stability you once knew is gone. There are totally different kinds of problems. The old ways of thinking and managing no longer work. And as you strive to keep up, you have no choice. You *have* to be creative.

Next comes the question of where you find the guidance you need to proceed on your uncharted path. Many Americans are turning to psychotherapy, hypnosis, yoga, body therapies, meditation, guided visualization, sensitivity training, and many other methods of developing their human potential.

They look to psychiatrists, behavioral scientists, counselors, and other experts in the field. But in all of what is now a substantial body of creative knowledge, seldom is there even a passing mention of the truest creativity of all — the arts. Personally, I don't understand how this can be. How can you discuss creativity without ever accessing the real, historically recognized expert, the artist?

The fact is that every living thing is creative. Plants grow into a glorious variety of sizes, shapes and natural arrangements. Animals respond in countless innovative ways to their environment. And as human beings, we all have the same, and more, innate capacity to be creative. Those of us we call artists are only those individuals who exercise their creativity to the fullest. It's all just a matter of degree.

Now, I'm not suggesting that everyone who wants to be creative must be an artist. I *am* suggesting that everyone who wants to be creative should be well acquainted with the arts. Works of art serve, not as goals, but as standards of creative excellence.

The Creativity Crisis

Let's take a quick look at how our society got into its "creativity crisis" in the first place, and how there came to be such a schism between the workaday world and the artistic experience.

The arts once played an integral role in the daily lives of men, women, and children. They still do in many societies. But in our society, the United States, music, dance, painting, all have been isolated and either placed on a pedestal or denigrated to valueless entertainment.

It is only since the industrial revolution that what we now call "the arts" have been separated from the rest of life. The Grecian Bowl we view with awe in the museum was once just another cereal dish. The decoration was not conceived separately from the object it decorated.

Before the machine age, all work involved imagination and creativity. It took imagination to design the first hunting tool. Down through history men and women have taken pride in everything they have created. Any so-called artistic merit was indistinguishable from its utilitarian purpose.

Today, alas, there is not only no time, but often no need, for craftsmanship. Many machine-made products are actually superior to those made by hand. But by thus excluding the creative process altogether, we have both unnecessarily degraded labor and inappropriately exalted art (to paraphrase Christopher Lasch).

For the past 200 years there has been no place for creativity in the industrial workplace. Those people in whom the creative urge refused to be stifled were forced outside the mainstream of economic productivity. Living either in the loft of poverty or the academic haven, they have been supported by an incestuous system of patronage and denied all meaningful contact with the broader market place. A few recent experiments with public art have underscored the wide gap that has grown between artists and society as a whole.

This gap, however, has not been caused only by the division of labor between "essential" and "nonessential." The new scientific method which arose in the 19th century provoked the even more unnatural separation of thinking from feeling. With the advent of the dispassionate, objective view of the world, the arts were further distanced by their connection with feelings and emotions. Cold logic was the key to progress; emotionalism was a sign of confusion and weakness.

It was Sigmund Freud who applied the goals of scientific control to the human mind. Plato, Aristotle and Seneca all saw the similarity between artists and the insane, attributing their respective visions and delusions to supernatural forces. Freud correctly redefined the supernatural as the unconscious mind — but continued to identify both imagination and hallucination as abnormal. According to his famous theory of psychoanalysis, the artistic and psychopathic processes are one and the same! Creativity, innovativeness and genius (he said) are all part of a long list of neuroses that need to be brought under control. Neuroscientists and biochemists see the function of the brain differently today, but the stigma is still attached to artists, the Bohemian painter the epitome of "infantile self-indulgence."

On the other hand, those who remained in the working world were also deprived of an important dimension of human life. Based on the Puritan ethic, work was functional in nature, unadorned by any pleasurable sensations. Later, around the turn of the century, the simplification and standardization of procedures known as the assembly line was the next logical step in this line of reasoning. As a result, not just the line workers, but those who manage them, all have been dominated by dull, monotonous, uninspired jobs. Only the artist has been left with any joy in his work — which only proves, perversely, that it isn't really work.

The public education system, designed to prepare students to perform well in regular, routinized employment, emphasizing explicit knowledges and vocationally-oriented skills, has successfully institutionalized these differences between artists and workers.

While "common art," that is, arts and crafts, popular music, dance and variety entertainment, are readily available for mass consumption, "high art" remains the almost exclusive possession of a cultivated minority. This minority is usually of the socially elite and economically privileged, the classes most likely to have the time and money required to gratify their refined tastes.

High art, in other words, has become a luxury of the rich, a frill of education, and a symbol of snobbery to the vast majority of Americans. No wonder that the business community, even as it faces a desperate need for change, gives no serious thought to the arts as models for the development of practical thinking skills.

Self-Expression in Everyday Life

Now maybe the time has come to change all that. I believe it is time to recognize our artists as members of the workforce, and at the same time to put the creative process back into the workplace. We have been out of touch with ourselves and each other for too long.

When our early leaders, notably John Adams and Benjamin Franklin, foresaw that our nation would rise to greatness upon the ladder of machines and industrialization, they erred in their misunderstanding of the arts and their fear that such "frivolities" would hamper progress. In their zeal for results, they forgot that even machines are based on dreams and creative emotions.

The germinal cell of creativity has been ignored, scorned as a nuisance, or forgotten altogether for so long that all that's left for us is a material shell. As human beings, we are left starved for a sense of self expression, but so out of practice that, today, wearing designer jeans or putting a new dressing on a lettuce and tomato salad seems expressive.

Nearly forty years ago, Eric Fromm predicted that, deprived of all joy and stimuli on the job, eventually people would be unable to work at all. What he didn't predict was that as a nation we would also lose our standing in international commerce. But so it is today, and so it may be for you, too.

So let's stop thinking of our professional artists as

emotionally unstable idlers, uniquely detached from real life, and their works "divinely inspired" rather than painstakingly, all too humanly, crafted. Let's also recognize that even amateur participation in the arts has value far greater than private enjoyment of a leisure time activity.

Let's also enlarge our understanding of the creative process. Having bypassed the arts, we have been left with a very narrow definition of intellectual creativity, aimed primarily at problem-solving. Thinking, reasoning, feeling, emotion and intellect are all interrelated, all part of a whole pattern. The many different kinds of mental abilities, skills and habits — perception, judgment, problem-solving, decision-making, organization, planning, analytical thinking, synthetic thinking — cannot be individually abstracted, nor can they all be run together willy-nilly.

Free Your Creative Spirit

The rest of what I have to say will be specifically about the nature of creativity and how you can regain and cultivate your God-given ability.

Webster says to create means "to bring into being; invest with new form; produce as a work." A tangible product is always based on the creative process. But the creative process does not always generate a tangible product.

Expressiveness can also be used as a tool. For example, you can't express yourself if you don't understand yourself; understanding yourself is the first step in understanding others; and understanding others is the key to successful interpersonal relations. Self-expression, then, is not just a passive release of pent-up emotions, it is the actual transformation of emotion into action. By the way, good theatre can teach you much about interpersonal expressiveness in action. So can a musical ensemble.

It is only recently that I realize how much I learned about human relations in my many years of chamber music playing. Anton Kuerti, a renowned concert pianist, says that playing music together is a "highly fulfilling social activity, combining the physical, emotional and intellectual domains; requiring much skill, cooperation and instant response, and perceiving how diverse parts can fit together perfectly, be they parts of a mechanism, a puzzle or a piece of music." Individual expression sensitively balanced with subordination to the group, this is teamwork at its best.

Of course, not all groups achieve this level of compatibility. Henny Youngman remarked of the musicians who worked with him, "Each of these boys is a soloist. If you don't believe me, listen to them when they try to play together."

Artists demonstrate the highest level of development, but all creative people share the following basic traits:

1. Openness to new ideas, new experiences, new

ways of doing things. As a creative person, you will question everything. You will practice what John Budd, vice president of corporate communications at Emhart Corporation, calls the "art of divine discontent." You will be curious, always asking, "What would happen if..." You will also ignore restraints and pre-established criteria (thus probably getting a reputation as a "difficult" person), and pay no attention to arguments such as, "We've never done that before..." "We're not ready for that..." "What we have is good enough..." "We tried it once..." "It costs too much..." "It's not our responsibility." Even "It won't work" will not affect you, the determined creator. You will always look first for the best possible outcome and then, as necessary, modify it to meet specific requirements or stay within prescribed boundaries.

2. As a creative person, you will be optimistic that for every problem there is a solution, and trusting that the best you have envisioned will prevail. Because of the depressing nature of work in our society, criticism and negativism are considered "smart." Positive, supportive people are "wimps." But the creative approach is to state a problem positively, think constructively, and know the right time for action will come. Your optimism will give you the strength to persist in the face of all difficulties; to persevere, no matter what the obstacles. But you will not be all "piss and vinegar"; you will know how to be patient, too. You will be self-disciplined and diligent, practice your skills daily, letting ideas ebb and flow, combining, adapting, manipulating, playing with them, knowing that the creative force takes its own time. You will not feel you have to fire off brilliant decisions at the drop of every hat.

3. Intrinsic motivation is a hallmark of creative people. You will be independent, self-sufficient and willing to take risks. Your idea of adventure will not be limited to buying a new Jeep. It is commonly believed that creative achievers consistently achieve. Actually, they fail many times. But you will not fear failure. In fact, you will find that you don't even think about it. Warren Bennis, professor of management at the University of Southern California, says creative people have tremendous self-confidence. This means that you will also be good at dealing with frustration, a frequent component of the creative process. As a creative person, if you are ever stuck in a traffic jam, you will take advantage of the opportunity to try out a new route. Incidentally, studies done by "behavioral geographers" show that if you always travel the same way, the brain starts to miss big chunks of reality. The creative process of finding a new route allows your old "animal instinct" to join forces with your newer human cortex — to the great satisfaction of both.

4. Additional terms which describe creative people are flexibility, fluidity, tolerance of ambiguity and analogous thinking. You will be able to shift your perspective and see more than one approach to a situation or problem. The "quick fix" mentality is alien to creativity; a general rule of thumb is to consider at least three alternatives. This requires farsightedness, the ability to see beyond the obvious, and above all, a certain distance from your own view. One way to develop this ability is to adopt the viewpoint of someone you know well. Then stretch further to a casual acquaintance. Later, you will be able to pick up and adapt ideas from complete strangers, and from books, tapes, television and other sources of impersonal information.

Goals are a mixed blessing to the creative person. Specific, measurable, relevant objectives, targets and deadlines are often counterproductive. Goals are to the creative process as dams are to a great river — they harness the power, but stop the flow. Goals are set judiciously by creative people.

You will have the ability to shift from one mode of thinking to another. You will verbalize, draw a picture, turn a birdsong into a melody, choreograph a dance from the movement of a lizard, write a poem about a rainbow, or make a logical arrangement of an odd collection of facts. You will be able to interpret a variety of symbols — words, music, mathematics — and use them interchangeably

Einstein expressed his physical theory of relativity, with its absence of fixed dimensions of time and space, in mathematical formulae. About the same time, Arnold Schoenberg introduced atonality, the absence of a fixed tonal center in music, in a string quartet. Now, I am using words of my choosing to convey these ideas to you. This is a creative exchange of symbolism.

As you progress with your creativity, you will gain a tolerance for ambiguity and uncertainty about the outcome of actions and decisions. You will be able to accept things the way they are, not the neat way you would like them to be. Not all differences have to be resolved; conflict is often a means to a new idea (which is still another mode of thinking, called dialectics).

Multiple choice, true-false, and other objective questions on standardized tests have convinced us that there is always a "right" answer. Creative people know better.

You will find yourself transferring knowledge, ideas or techniques from one situation to another. Agatha Christie's elderly sleuth, Miss Jane Marple, was frequently reminded of someone or something from her old village life — which always helped her solve the immediate crime.

You might start developing this skill by picking up an unfamiliar magazine. Read the incidental information, the acknowledgements, sketches of the writers, ads, etc. Learn to perceive the editorial "slant," interpret or translate it into your own terms, understand its significance and apply it to yourself.

5. One of the most important attributes of the creative person is astute observation. You will be able to "see" things that no one else can see. When Michelangelo entered a sculpture contest, he arrived a day late and found only a few, misshapen pieces of marble left. He looked them over, selected one and carved his immortal "David." Asked how he did it, he said, "I just looked at the marble, saw David in it, and carved around him." You will also look at even familiar objects and see something different than you ever saw before. With your "wide angle" vision, you will absorb a myriad of details of sights, sounds, movement, making interesting and valuable connections within the diversity of your experiences.

6. But creativity is not all looking outward. Receptivity to internal stimuli is needed too. This is known as intuition. Popularly described as following a hunch rather than using logic, intuition is not something you hide behind when logic fails; it is a system in its own right. It includes your education, training, the total of everything you have learned, felt, experienced. The well-known "Eureka!" factor, the insight that comes in a blinding flash, appears only after extensive preparation, careful scrutinizing of facts and information, the weighing of evidence and a (usually) long incubation, all in your unconscious. Like other skills, intuition improves with practice. You could, for instance, try to foretell the future. If you're meeting friends after work, try to guess what they'll be wearing. When you talk to a new person on the telephone, imagine what he or she looks like. Before you open the mailbox, try to predict what correspondence you will receive. You will later, of course, verify your prediction or your hunch against available facts. You will test it for accuracy and value and if it is found wanting, you will discard it. But you will never abandon it just because of unfounded "logical" doubts and uncertainties, and you will certainly never dismiss a correct hunch as just a "coincidence."

7. I have left originality for last because it is not really a learned skill or ability. Actually, originality is simply your own personality. There is no talent involved; you are indubitably original. Every snowflake is original; every fingerprint is original; every expression of your motives and values created by you, is original. What you might have to do is to consciously free yourself from fixed ideas you have accumulated and break out of the conventional thinking that you have adoped. Otherwise, originality is like happiness: the more you chase after it, the more it eludes you. In fact, the obsessive search for originality is the surest denial of it.

The Delicacy of Creativity

Before I finish, I'd like to tell you one more story about what, if we're not very careful, can happen to a budding creative spirit.

A first grade class was going to have its first art lesson. "Children," said the teacher, "I want you to paint a picture, and I want you to do anything you want." One small boy was especially eager as he prepared his paper and paints. With joyful anticipation he painted a flower, titling it "Daisy." It was a most remarkable daisy, with a purple stem, orange leaves, and a veritable rainbow of multi-colored petals. Proudly, he showed his creation to the teacher. "Oh, that's lovely," she assured him, "but it doesn't look like a real daisy, does it? Here, let me help you." And so she patiently showed him how to paint a green stem, and white petals, and a bright yellow center. At first the boy was disappointed, but he tried to please, and with his teacher's help, he gradually learned to paint excellent daisies. And he went on to roses, violets and all kinds of flowers. He never quite regained the wonderful enthusiasm he had had at first, but everyone told him what a fine young artist he was. And so the semesters went by. Then one day a new teacher came to the school. "Children," said the teacher, "I want you to paint a picture, and I want you to do anything you want." With a rush, all the old excitement came back to the boy. Eagerly, he selected his materials, and with joyful anticipation, he painted his old favorite, "Daisy." It was a lovely daisy, with a green stem, white petals, and bright yellow center...

Creativity is a delicate, complex process. It is a process that engages your whole being. It requires intellect, sensibility and stamina. By no means, however, do these requirements exempt the "other abled." When Pope John Paul II visited Los Angeles in 1987, the entire nation took to its heart a young man who, armless since birth, inspired us with his great courage and talent as he played the guitar with his feet. Iztak Perlman, one of today's world class violinists, is confined to a wheelchair. A whole school of art was founded by a paraplegic who held a paint-brush in her teeth to produce beautiful paintings.

Learn from the Masters

In many other ways, men and women throughout history have left their legacy of creativity in mechanical inventions, scientific discoveries, religious thought and technological innovations.

Still, the best examples of the creative process are what we call works of art. The people who produce these works may or may not, themselves, understand the process. And if they understand it, they may or may not be able to articulate it. This, then is not a bumper-sticker exhortation to "take an artist to lunch." It is rather an invitation to each of you who seeks to free your creative spirit to learn from the masters.

Great artists demonstrate creativity at its finest. They both reflect and shape our ideals. They are both recorders of the old and innovators of the new. There is no substitute for direct participation in their vision.

Finally, the experts agree, creativity is catching! By spending time with other creative people, increasing your understanding of the great masterpieces of artistic creativity and, above all, by carefully studying the working methods and techniques of accomplished artists, you can take *your* rightful place in the creative world.

Tom Wheeler
DAPLUS Company
13640 Poway Springs Rd.
Poway,CA 92064
(619) 748-6297 (619) 748-6296

Tom Wheeler

Tom graduated from Villanova University in 1960 with a B.A. degree. He started working for IBM in 1963 and has spent the past twenty-five years actively involved in computer design and development. He has been involved with many advanced computer projects in large and small systems. One such involvement was the original IBM Personal Computer design task force.

In 1984 Tom joined G.E.Calma as Vice President for Advanced Systems, where he was responsible for designing Calma's Advanced engineering systems. He is currently president of DAPLUS which focuses on system design problems. Currently Tom works with large corporations on computer systems questions with a concentration on work-station designs.

Tom is a member of professional organizations including New York Academy of Science, IEEE, IEEE Computer Society, World Future Society, Association of Computing Machinery, National Computer Graphics Association, and the Neural Network Society. He is chairman of the American Electronics Association Education Committee for San Diego.

Tom has been active in youth activities, holding many volunteer positions with the Boy Scouts of America. His most recent job in that area was National Chairman of Science and Engineering for the Exploring program.

He is listed in a number of biographical listings: Who's Who in the East, Who's Who in the West, Who's Who in the World, Who's Who in American Technology, *and* The Directory of Distinguished Americans.

Tom has given and published talks and professional papers on computers and design automation in over twenty countries. A couple of talks that have received wide general interest are, The Mythical, Magical, Mysterious World of Computing, *and* Trends in Computer Technology. *Tom has recently completed a book for McGraw Hill entitled* Computers and Engineering Managers.

Creativity in Large Companies

By Tom Wheeler

*"Every great advance in science has issued
from a new audacity of imagination."*
 - Mosaic at Bronx School of Science

Have you ever paused to imagine the creative environment in America's largest corporations? Unlike images of the helter-skelter laboratories of the great inventors like Edison and Bell, we imagine well polished organizations fostering creativity with modern equipment. Creative imaginations benefit from these terrific surroundings, but they also suffer from organizational structures which stifle innovation. For more than twenty plus years, I have been privileged to manage in this modern creative world. During those years I benefited from the top support and became frustrated with bureaucratic procedures hampering the creativity they were supposed to stimulate.

My adventure began in the middle of the design flurry of large IBM computer systems in the 1960's and 1970's. After many such projects within IBM, I experienced a new breath of fresh air as a member of the design task force for the Personal Computer. After a number of other efforts, I found myself again leading a design group within the General Electric organization. Each experience provided additional lessons about the ways of managing creative genius in large companies.

I am often reminded of the great Leonardo da Vinci and the patrons who helped insure his success. DaVinci experienced many frustrations of modern inventors and also many advantages of well endowed patrons. Throughout the middle ages creative people turned to wealthy benefactors to support artistic and scientific endeavors, while today inventors turn to venture capitalists or the more secure but often frustrating environment of a large corporation or government agency.

The Process

In corporations the development process is well bounded by formal schedules. Products are determined by their financial justifications within the framework of announcement and delivery dates. Staffs often challenge products until they are announced so we often found ourselves rushing to announce projects to secure them from further attacks. The safest project was the one announced and anticipated by customers.

Schedules could also lead the manager to a period of frustration. I am reminded of a skilled designer who was responsible for pivotal software. His peers had completed their coding while the designer worked on design. The manager almost had a nervous breakdown as management pressed for the product status and he could see no results. Finally in the last few days the designer coded a product that worked correctly the first time.

Leonardo's creativity existed in a world between the inventor and the artist. In some senses the world of Edison was similar but as we moved into modern years, the innovative genius of an Edison has often been replaced by creative teams working to produce complex products. Once the idea is created, support groups provide detailed drawings and verify correctness. Yet in the midst of this team effort, I have found designers with that special mystique which marks unique and winning products.

Computers have become the tools which enable the cognitive capability of designers to meld with automation and provide new thought processes. Although manual computing was always fundamental to invention, automation has greatly modified our capabilities to create. We can easily imagine ancient engineers creating pyramids with scratched calculations in the Egyptian sands. The complex needs of modern society have placed increasing accuracy requirements on designers. A faulty design in a jet engine would ruin the day for a number of people. The ancient sands have been molded into silicon chips to provide the tablet for our high speed calculations.

Design Environment

Once I had the opportunity to give a talk at the Bronx school of Science. In a mosaic above the lobby there is a challenge for students, which should be shared with all designers. "Every great advance in science has issued from a new audacity of imagination." It is this audacity of imagination we seek in large organizations.

As managers we must develop an environment stimulating creativity. Ideas can occur at the most inconvenient times, often in the relaxing atmosphere of play or meditation or even more relaxing moments. Designs can often emerge while cutting wood or simply relaxing in a canoe. Environmental factors include the cognitive, physical, institutional and external elements which can alter individual creativity. Understanding this environment begins with individuals and proceeds to the team which in large projects often consists of hundreds of people.

Cognition refers to the ability to know and then

create. This thought process turns a wild idea into a design and eventually a product. Creative thought begins with the cognitive self which springs from individual problem-solving skills. Hofstadter in his thought-provoking book entitled, *Goedel, Escher, Bach* pointed out that computers "catalyzed the convergence of three previously disparate areas: the theory of axiomatic reasoning, the study of mechanical computation, and the psychology of intelligence." (Hofstadter 1979)

Technical creativity can spring from many different disciplines. When we developed IBM's mainframes in the 1960's, we had a team of developers from fifty-seven nations assigned to the Endicott, New York laboratory. Their background was as diverse as their languages. Music majors teamed with electrical engineers while philosophy majors mixed with mathematicians to produce the highly successful product lines. Each intelligent person brought a perspective making the entire product lines stronger. Computer science was born from a chaotic mix of many different disciplines and continues to benefit from multiple views of problems.

I have learned that cognitive individuals benefit from periods of quiet very similar to that found in monastic environments. Reflection permits ideas to grow and concepts to flourish. The designer is often inundated with new information, but it is only through periods of inner silence that facts are synthesized into new designs. Information has been described as unconnected items such as dates, names, or other data. Knowledge is the assembly of these items with connections between them. Creativity springs first from knowledge.

As an active design manager, I have had to balance the roles of designer and manager in a constant trade-off between demands of product schedules and creative behavior. Constantly I was faced with questions about creativity and whether it can exist in an environment tortured by constant pressures. Can invention be scheduled or is invention without schedule a form of random movement? Can an environment be created to stimulate the purest form of cognition while responding to the constant needs of large organizations? How can we build creative environments in a bureaucracy?

The creative person must reach a product definition which is not only possible, but also meets the requirements of a market. Product priorities can eliminate truly great ideas but also place reality criteria on flaky proposals. The hard measurements of profitability help eliminate useless bells and whistles as we move from many possible alternatives to the ones reflecting development and profit realities.

Designers create universes which work according to their own unique set of rules. This power is both rewarding and frustrating, as designers are faced with two confusing and opposite forces. The engineer believes there are few limits to the possible. Technology and knowledge seem to guarantee perfect machines, but history continually emphasizes problems and mistakes which disprove perfect machines. Experts question the need for tests until the first problem arises demonstrating their ideal product is something less. Design errors trouble only the true egoists, because they believe such problems can never occur.

Physical science and human constraints limit the creators and their universe, so management must balance between the possible and impossible. Invention moves in steps built on previous knowledge with alternatives that can be verified and accelerated by computer. In the case of computers the deeper the knowledge base the higher probability of success.

Thomas Jefferson pointed to the effects of negative intelligence which can limit creativity. Many have observed a negative group dynamic takes place when a dullard is introduced to the team. The team spends time dealing with the lack of ideas so negative intelligence causes results inferior to total team skills. Satisfaction with working relationships have demonstrable effects on design teams. It is necessary to avoid the situation where designers spend twenty percent of their time working on design problems and the remainder working on themselves.

Ideas

I have found conventional theories of ideas useful in understanding creativity. Designs pass through a cycle in which a design proposal or conjecture is made by one designer. As others think of technical reasons the design will not work or must be modified, they pose alternatives creating the next step toward the completed idea. Popper (Popper-1962) spoke of this cycle as a conjecture-refutation cycle which constantly results in higher synthesis. This process was formalized through a series of design meetings, called walk-thrus, in which peers evaluate correctness of specific designs. Creative ideas are polished through these design meetings with intelligent and often strong willed individuals. As feasibility is challenged a deeper technology results, which opens new problems, but finally produces a product definition and workable design.

Creative thought is largely an organization of elementary information presented in some serial fashion. We build from these processes as we expose them to new hypotheses with the resultant step toward design. In an organization process formality can create a structured or simulation environment which assists design. Techniques using both structured definition and simulation have proved to be useful to engineering teams in their design efforts.

New design cycles begin with a period of intense research into older techniques or academic studies on the subject. This period of self-instruction is followed by a period in which ideas literally pour forth. I am reminded of the purgation and illumination stages found in mystical writings. Knowledge continues to expand as we move through the final stages of design. Synthesis is the most gratifying stage for the designers as the design takes shape in a running model or prototype. Throughout design a thought discipline can enhance creativity as long as it does not get in the way. The design will be paced by managers aware of the balance between competent and novice designers. Creative teams benefit from effective communications. A network helps accelerate the healthy interaction between new ideas. Computer connections have permitted these connections across the world. For example, Digital Equipment Corporation from Boston uses a world-wide network between design teams to exchange ideas. Engineers can sit at a workstation in Maynard and use satellite communications to talk to engineers across the world. Ideas can be shared between plants in Massachusetts and Ireland in a matter of minutes. Rapid electronic communications now permit worldwide teams of designers to share a part in a common design. Team creativity has become a global reality.

Physical Environment

Thoreau once commented that, "Solitude is not measured by the miles of space that intervene between a man and his fellows." Yet often as I stroll through the halls at Jefferson's home in Monticello, Virginia, his genius seems to spring from every niche of the great house. Inventions which made his life easier amidst the rigors of colonial Virginia still demand our admiration today. Many of these inventions and perhaps many of his creative ideas on government, spring from the reflective solitude of this retreat.

I have also found myself in many corporate laboratories around the world. These laboratories are designed to foster the creativity of the designers, but their structures often are very different. We closely formulated plans for the IBM programming laboratory in Santa Teresa, California. Our studies pointed to the requirement for facilities which fostered the expression of new ideas. Conference rooms were essential for team interaction, but so too was space for individual designers. The building provided sufficient space for each knowledge worker as well as special wiring for their computer tools.

By sharp contrast, the IBM laboratory in Hursley England is located in the old and stately Hursley House. This land, which dates back to the early kings of England, is reminiscent of Monticello yet it was the design center for the Spitfire fighter during the second World War and is now used to design modern workstations. The designer can still wander the large grounds and contemplate a design while enjoying the beauty of the English countryside and listening to the bells of Winchester Cathedral.

When I visited the laboratory in Cupertino where the Apple team designed the Macintosh, I was struck by the significant differences. A ping-pong table and piano were the first items to strike my eye emphasizing informality of the design environment. Even here computers were connected to provide the design team a creative environment with modern tools.

The great General Electric laboratory at Schnectady is reminiscent again of Monticello. This old building nestled in northern hardwoods and over-looking the river gives a sense of serenity. The powerful creativity emanating from this laboratory becomes obvious when one finds it has produced more patents than any other lab in the United States.

Personal computers have changed our creative world. I have found them being used for many artistic creativity as well as technical designs. Artists use them to compose music, write poetry, or even create paintings. These desktop workstations have become doorways into worlds of creativity unimagined only a few years ago. Newton once pointed to our ability to stand on the shoulders of genius as we move forward to the future. Today we can literally find those shoulders of previous genius folded into the computer. Cognition benefits from easy access to information, which grows tomorrow's ideas.

Institutional or Organizational

The company, division, and department creates conditions stimulating creativity. Creative ideas map closely to the organizational structures. If the organization changes it is often necessary to change the linkages between design groups. Computers can be used to maximize the engineer's attention to the job and facilitate both communication through the organization and response to bureaucratic processes.

The bureaucracy can build barriers which are frustrating to creative people. These can be simple barriers which limit the access to communications or computer equipment, or more subtle such as complex accounting rules which consume time on the part of the creative person. In the personal computer example, we found that the system had grown to create barriers to rapid shipment of new products. A part of the magic of the personal computer was the speed in which good ideas could be delivered to the market.

Great ideas flow from positive organizations which give meaning to individual inventors. Negative dynamics generated from uncertainty slows projects and hampers new ideas. Creative people become very concerned about negative forces such as moves, organizational changes, and loss of budget. These necessary personnel shifts must occur rapidly to minimize their adverse effects. Like the patrons of daVinci, the manager must shield the creative genius from trivia and help stimulate their ideas. The manager pierces inertia and creates a positive atmosphere to design and develop products.

Career-Long Learning

Fortunately most creative people have a continual thirst for new knowledge, since technical disciplines in particular are constantly changing. The designer's intellectual climate begins long before college and is usually fostered in the home. The child who is taught to read and to challenge, becomes a good candidate for creativity. Challenging learning conditions provide a base for schooling, but much more, provide the questing mind with a sounding board for their new ideas.

The personal computer team constantly chose avenues different from the standard to solve the problems.

Organizationally we often place people in slots which define our creative expectations. Surprise sets in when we find many who were defined out of the creative team actually provide many unique and different ideas. The young innovative engineer often provides the fresh viewpoint which is the breakthrough for a product, yet we often assign the college grad to menial support tasks. The schools often counter creativity by applying organizational methodology to the creative person. Thus the frustrations of bureaucracy arise early. The story is told about Einstein dropping out of school early to avoid constant senseless conflict with exams.

The excitement and atmosphere of a creative team is developed by managers who build and refresh their designers. As it turns out the half life of engineering knowledge is very brief. According to the American Society of Engineering Education, ten years after graduation about half of engineering knowledge is out of date. In the rapidly changing electronic area the half-life of accurate knowledge is probably about three years. Every two and half years a new generation of technology is making faster computers available with additional functions.

Technical learning never ceases since there is constant change. Engineers must constantly learn the new aspects of their disciplines to keep large design teams creative. This is a split responsibility since the individual professional must continually seek more information and management must assist the process. It is especially important that the key designers receive a periodic refresher in related fields. This can be accomplished both by formal courses and rapid access to information on technology changes. The new techniques using computer aided information libraries can keep the designers up to speed. Intensive university seminars, in-house video tapes and satellite instruction have all been employed to help stimulate career-long learning.

The computer offers a terrific way to stay abreast of latest technology. The computer network can be used to broadcast information about technology changes. Engineering knowledge has become more organized over the past 100 years. The challenge to the management team is to use the most effective tools in insuring a strong professional learning environment for the engineering team. Management needs to plan and provide resources for career-long learning.

Conclusions

A number of friends have noted that the title of this chapter is a contradiction, since they believe creativity is impossible in large corporations. It is certainly hampered by very political management and by bureaucracies which continually deter effective ideas. We have shown creative ideas can be fostered in spite of large companies through careful management and cooperation of the designers. Managers will live in a world of frustration and satisfaction as large companies try to foster creativity.

In this world of rapid change, company and even national success depends on stimulating new and better ideas. It is the creative genius of designers who assure continued leadership by making the design world a stimulating and real environment for new inventions. The power of the creative mind must be unleashed for our continued successes.

We are in a world of constant change with new designs being created daily. Although many believe we can envisage where technology will take us, I am constantly reminded of a quote from John Dewey that, *"Every thinker puts some portion of an apparently stable world in peril and no one can predict what will emerge in its place."* The creative individual contributes to our world of uncertainty and promise. It is to the promise that we must direct our attention and hopes.

> **"Knowing others is wisdom;**
> **Knowing the self is enlightenment."**
> - Lao Tsu, *Tao Te Ching*

REFERENCES

Hofstadter, D.R.: *Goedel, Escher, Bach*, Vintage Books, New York, NY, 1979.

Popper, K.R., *Conjectures and Refutations*, Basic Books Inc., New York, 1962.

Sculley, J., with Byrne, J.A., *Oyssey, Pepsi to Apple...* , Harper & Row, NY,1987, p184.

Simon, H. A., *Scientific Discovery and the Psychology of Problem Solving,* from Mind and Cosmos, edited by R.G.Colodny, University of Pittsburgh Press, Pittsburgh, PA.,1966.

Janice Baylis
P.O. Box 5084
Huntington Beach, CA 92646
(213) 598-5342

Janice Baylis

Janice Baylis, Ph.D. earned her B.A. in Education from Occidental College. She had a long, successful teaching career as a reading specialist. Janice did intense, self-directed study in the area of dreams. Included were classes from nationally known dream experts such as Drs. Knippner, Progoff, Rossi, Kohn, and Hart. Through the Association for Research and Enlightenment, she studied with Drs. Puryear and Reed, Hugh Lynn Cayce, Edgar Evans Cayce, Scott Sparrow and others.

After much dream work based on life experiences and empirical evidence, Janice earned her M.A. in Psychology from Pepperdine University and her Ph.D. in Psychology from Columbia-Pacific University.

For years she has taught classes and workshops in dream study. Her students, from all walks of life, furnished the dream material for her book Sleep On It! The Practical Side of Dreaming. *Dr. Baylis' eclectic approaches and teaching methods provided the material for* Dream Dynamics and Decoding: An Interpretation Manual, *her workable "do-it-yourself" book.*

Retired from teaching, Janice now writes and lectures about the practical value of dreams. Janice tells interesting, often incredible dream examples of practical dream guidance and ways to understand dream messages.

She is a member of International Association for the Study of Dreams, Dream Educators' Network, and MENSA Toastmasters of Long Beach.

SLEEP ON IT!
The Practical Side of Dreaming

By Janice Baylis

*"To those who are awake there is one ordered universe
common to all, whereas in sleep each man turns away
from this world to one of his own."*
- Heraclitus

Amazing

This true story of a night dream that solved a problem—before we even knew we had the problem—

explains why I value dreams. For most people this incident is a "grabber." It started me on my years of dream study.

When I was a young mother and teacher, I drove sixty miles round-trip to work every day. I took my three sons with me. After surgery a fellow teacher, Mabel Olsen, asked me to pick her up part way to school to shorten her long drive. We chose a parking lot in front of three small stores as the spot to leave her car.

We met there at 7:00 a.m. daily. One morning, two weeks later, before I left my house for our meeting place, she phoned and said, "Let's not meet there anymore. I feel the store owners may not like my car in their lot all day. Let's leave my car around the corner on the residential street."

"Okay with me," I said.

So that morning I drove past our usual meeting place. While Mabel was getting into my car we heard an enormous crash. As we drove by our previous meeting spot we discovered that a small plane had crashed. There it was in the very corner of the parking lot where we had been meeting!

I stopped the car, stared at Mabel, and asked, "How did you know?"

"I dreamed it last night," she replied. "But I didn't tell you because I thought you might think it silly to pay attention to a dream. Besides, I wasn't sure it would really happen."

No planes had taken off in the early morning during the two weeks we had used that parking lot.

Yet, some part of Mabel's mind must have noticed that behind the row of windbreaker eucalyptus trees, there was a small, private airstrip. Her intuition and ESP went to work in the night and sent her a prodromic (warning) dream.

Because I had a teaching career at the time, dreams simply became a fascinating hobby for me. The fascination with dreams, especially their application to practical, daily living has increased over the years. Now that I'm retired from teaching, I like to help others by acquainting them with this individual resource — their own dreams.

This article will deal with only one aspect of dreaming, CREATIVITY, which is the making of something new. Creativity is only one thing that dreams facilitate. Dreams do many other equally important things.

Do I really mean to say that dreams are not just the mind relaxing into mild craziness, or just showing our emotional states, or just rehashing and filing the daily data intake? Do I really mean to say dreams can offer solutions to problems, creative breakthroughs and practical guidance?

The craziness is actually our lack of understanding symbolic and/or pictorial language. The "emotions only" theory stems from psychology's emphasis on this aspect and the use of dreams to resolve conflicts. The dream mind often turns to daily life in choosing symbols/pictures for its messages. This leads some people to think dreams are just a rehash of the day's experiences. However, I really do mean to say that dreams may offer solutions to problems, creative breakthroughs and practical guidance.

Nobel Prize-Winning Dreams

Niels Bohr, Danish physicist and Nobel laureate, discovered that atomic structure resembles a solar system. "The Bohr Atomic Model" first revealed to mankind the atomic nucleus surrounded by orbiting electrons much like the sun is surrounded by orbiting planets. Where did Niels Bohr get this realization? He often related that it was in a dream when he saw a visualization of the intra-atomic arrangement. He stated that in his dream he witnessed "the superhuman showmanship of elementary particles with the electrons speeding around the nuclei in their orbital paths."

Otto Lowei had his Nobel Prize dream three nights in succession. While studying the human nervous system, he dreamed of an experiment with two frogs. He scribbled notes about the dream in the dark. Next morning he could not read the notes nor could he remember the dream. That night he had the same experience. When the dream returned on the third night, he got out of bed, went to his laboratory and performed the experiment as dreamed.

He electrically activated the heart nerve of one frog. A small amount of chemical formed on the nerve ending. He transferred this chemical (acetycholine) to the heart nerve of a second frog. That frog's nerve responded to the chemical by sending an impulse. Based on this experiment and proof that nerve impulses are transmitted both electrically and chemically, Otto Lowei received the 1936 Nobel Prize in Physiology.

Yet another Nobel Prize winner, the chemist Fredrick Kekule, credited his breakthrough insight to a dream experience. He tells the story of one important dream which he had when he fell asleep on a London omnibus:

"I saw atoms flicker. I always imagined them as eternally moving, but I had never been able to visualize their way of motion and relative arrangement. However, I saw two of them forming a small pair, two of these pairs forming a larger unit which in turn combined again into ever larger units, all of them rushing and turning. I awoke."

That evening he sketched the images which had appeared to him in his dream and the theory of closed atom chains was born.

A second dream, which Kekule had while studying to determine the structure of the benzene molecule, he reported this way:

"I was writing in my notebook, but my work appeared unsatisfactory. I just turned the chair around and drifted into a half-sleep. My mental eyes were able to perceive large manifold structures. Long rows, tightly knit, all in motion like a snake, turning and twisting and, 'Lo! What is that?' One of the snakes got hold of its own tail and scornfully rolled about in front of my eyes. The benzene ring! With the speed of lightning I awoke. I spent the balance of the night working out my hypothesis based on this dream experience."

Dream Artistic Creativity

Robert Louis Stevenson was working on a story intended to depict the dual nature of Man's personality (in psychological terms the persona and the shadow). He submitted a manuscript to his publisher but it was rejected. Two nights after the rejection Stevenson dreamed three scenes and the central plot to his now famous story, "The Strange Case of Dr. Jekyll and Mr. Hyde."

Jean Depre', French painter of "Pieta," reported this dream experience: While thinking about exactly where to position the figure of Christ, he fell asleep. In a dream he saw the composition and placement of the entire grouping of Christ and the disciples. His famous painting reproduces the image as seen in his dream.

Anton Rubenstein's Third Piano Concerto is his musical rendition of a visual dream experience. He reported it thusly:

"I found myself in a temple where the various instruments of an orchestra seem to have gathered, with the piano contributing seriously. The orchestral instruments subjected the piano to a difficult examination and they forced him to play different melodies and accords; then they announced in a firey tone that the piano cannot be considered as being one of them any more. The deep tones of the piano seized upon this occasion and began to cry bitterly. Then the piano collected itself bravely, declaring that it was going to create for itself its own orchestra. This statement made the other instruments so angry that they pushed the piano out of the door."

Genius of The Common Man

A teacher dreamed a design for a teaching aid. Here is her dream report:

"I was looking through a book. The pages were divided in half horizontally. The top half told and illustrated the story symbolically as it would appear in any book. The bottom half told and illustrated the story as it would appear if interpreted or translated into its real life meaning."

The teacher tried this and it worked out very well for teaching the psychological meaning of fairy tales.

An interior decorator reported this dream experience which led to the development of a main element in her individualizing of decor. It is an idea uniquely her own:

"I saw some window displays in homes and

businesses. Each window display was designed to express the personality, occupation or hobby of the resident, executive or business. I saw two examples in detail. One showed a scope and sequence flow chart in colors on the glass. The other was of a skier. I realized in the dream that the design should cover 20-40 percent of the window and leave 60-80 percent blank to allow light in. The more covered area, the more white was used in the design. Some designs seemed to have three dimensional elements."

Business Dreams

Mrs. Pansy Essman literally dreamed up a thriving business. She and her daughter got soaked giving the newborn granddaughter her first bath. The water terrified the baby. That night the grandmother, Mrs. Essman, dreamed.

"I dreamed about bathing a baby. I dreamed I went to my closet and pulled out a pillow-like piece of sponge that conformed to the baby's body. I placed the baby in it and bathed her. She laughed and splashed and her bath was a pleasure. The dream was so vivid, I woke up and realized that I had found the answer to the problem many mothers face with newborns."

Six months later she had found the right sponge-like material and her business was started. Pansy Ellen Products, Inc. began with the Pansyette Infant Bath Aid. She gave up her assembly line job to be president and run the business, manufacturing 20,000 bath aids per month. *(Reprinted by Permission of National Enquirer)*

Carl Duisberg was the director of the IG-Farben Co., manufacturers of paint. One day he fell asleep at his desk. His secretary came and woke him to go to an important meeting. He told the secretary what he had been dreaming. Later that day he called an impromptu meeting of his chemists to explain the dream which had contained a process to produce a special, superior blue paint pigment. The chemists tried out the process detailed in the dream, which resulted in a new paint that was a big money maker for the company and for Mr. Duisberg.

Conrad Hilton was interested in buying a company which was up for sale on a silent auction basis. He had submitted his bid the evening before closing time. That night he dreamed of a certain three place number. He says he saw the figure with his mind's eye while asleep. He awoke in the middle of the night still remembering the number. He felt that, with three zeros added, it was the figure he should have submitted as a bid. In the morning he changed his bid to the dream figure. He was the winning bidder, beating the nearest competitor by only $2,000.00. A few years later he sold that company for a two million dollar profit!

Sometimes good business guidance concerns what

not to do; that is how Millie's dreams helped her.

Millie was a widow in California. Soon after her husband died, Millie wondered what to do with the insurance money to best provide for the rest of her life. Having seen many fortunes made in California real estate she began to think about investing in land. While reading a magazine one day an advertisment for land in Australia caught her eye.

She met with the salesman. He explained that this land on the western side of Australia was presently wheat growing farmland. He mentioned that western Australia was the prime growth area echoing America's pioneer day slogan, "Go west, young man, go west." He felt this land would soon be ready to subdivide for housing. Last he explained a leverage system whereby a large group of people could each put in a relatively small amount of money and combine it to create big buying power.

She told him it sounded very good but she wanted to sleep on it. Millie was an accomplished dream incubator. She knew how to ask her dreams for direct help on a given problem or question. (I'll explain this process later.) That night Millie asked her dreams to comment on this Australian land investment.

First she dreamed that she saw a vast wheat field. A tree grew in the middle of the field. Then a hand appeared and picked peanuts off the tree. Writing this in her dream journal Millie recognized it as a dream picture of something someone might say. The growth there will only yield "peanuts" — a slang expression for "not very much money."

Millie had another dream later that night:

"I saw a man I know named Mr. Myers give some money to a young school boy I know whose name is J. West. He was sent to deliver the money to an office. On the way a gang of bigger boys jumped him and took most of the money. He arrived with just a little money, not quite empty handed."

Millie knew that much good dream interpretation comes from working with words written in dream journal recording. Mr. Myers, she felt, was a dream pun meaning "my ears." If she went by what she had heard, the plan sounded good, and she would put money into the idea of, "Go west, young man, go west." But in the dream the young man, West, had lost most of the money to a gang of bigger boys.

She called the salesman and told him she'd decided not to invest with his land company. Later at a party she found herself talking to a realtor. She asked him about the leverage system involved. His comments were to the effect that the company officials (big boys) usually take the main profits and the individual investors gain very little.

What Do We *Not* Need for Creativity

We do not need certain attitudes and thought processes that block innovative, creative thinking. Dreams are a good way around these thinking hang-ups. Dreams are not the only way around them, but dreams do tend to side-step certain attitudes more or less naturally.

One group of creative thinking inhibitors hinges on our comfort zone:

• Breaking the rules is usually not comfortable, so we tend not to explore or discover possibilities that are outside known rules, not "according to the book." It is safe to break rules while dreaming.

• Appearing foolish to others is uncomfortable, but if you try something foolish in a dream — who's to know? A foolish idea may ignite your mind. Many of today's realities were only "foolish ideas" a few years ago.

• Ambiguous situations that can be interpreted in more than one way make most people uncomfortable. But a puzzling dream may cause you to question some of your assumptions and thus lead to a variety of new ideas.

• In waking life too many people are satisfied when they find one workable solution to a problem. They tend to stop looking, if they find any right answer. Yet, a *better* right answer may be just a dream away.

• In this age of specialization people seldom look outside their own field of expertise. This is a form of tunnel vision. Dreams with their metaphors and analogies help widen our field of vision. We may discover relationships that are adaptable to our own field of problems.

Another set of creative thinking inhibitors is perpetuated by school and parental training:

• "Be practical, be logical, don't play around," we are told. These are good qualities — sometimes. But in dreams we can produce ideas which as yet have no basis in experience. The initial or embryonic stage of creativity requires an open mind, and elliptical or even fantastic thinking. Practical, evaluative judgement and modification come later in the creative process. Everyone knows that dreams are not bound by strict, conscious logic. This can be very useful!

• "If necessity is the mother of invention, play is the father." This quote from Roger von Oech's *Whack on the Side of the Head* says it all.

• "Don't make mistakes," we're admonished. But, how many wrong materials did Edison try before he made a tungsten filament for the light bulb? Mistakes offer useful negative feedback. Sometimes dreams also take this approach, demonstrating the potential results of what won't work. What a time and effort saver to try it out in a dream.

Creative, innovative behaviour is often trained out of children. Children are encouraged to:

Stick to the rules.
Stick to routine.
Stick to known facts.
Stick to the logical.
Stick to the certain/safe.
Stick to group assumptions.
Stick to your field.
Stick to the conventional.

The trouble with that is that we all get stuck!

Dreams are free to:
>Try out "what if's."
>Try out other fields or specialties.
>Try out metaphors.
>Try out breaking the rules.
>Try out new ideas.
>Try out dropping obsolete ideas/rules.
>Try out risks, physical and social.

Don't be stuck with a self-concept that says, "Me, I'm not creative." Make note of your dreams in a dream journal, and discover your synthesizing, thinking capabilities.

What Do We Need for Creativity?

• We need less inhibited thinking as discussed in the previous section.

• We need facts, experiences, and research as bait on the hook to dip into creative intuition.

• We need motivation, a goal, or a solution we are seeking.

• We need an incubation period. Creative intuition is a faculty of mind not really under direct conscious control. It works subconsciously and surfaces after a time. Intuitive insights and inspirations come from the incubation of information in the subconscious mind, perhaps in a dream.

• Then, naturally, we need confident follow-through.

Directed Dream Incubation

Most of the dream examples I've used are instances of spontaneous, undirected incubation and creativity. It happens! The elements for creativity were there and the insights resulted without the active planning of the dreamer. But dream creativity does not need to be left to chance. It can be planned and directed. When it is, it's usually called dream incubation. Remember, I mentioned that Millie's dreams about the Australian land investment were deliberatly incubated.

The Elements and Sequence for Dream Incubation:

Conscious Investigation -*Waking Input*

Fact gathering, related experiences, consideration of alternatives come in at this initial stage. This goes on naturally in our daily lives but it can be more effective if it is planned and directed. This material needs to be reviewed before going to sleep on a night when a dream incubation is planned.

Motivation/Focus -*Incubation Phrase or Question*

This is usually there as a goal, as a problem to be solved or as an understanding to be gained. When this is part of a planned dream incubation, it must be formed into a phrase or question directed to the dream mind. Write this phrase or question into your dream journal before going to bed. Then focus on it and repeatedly say it to yourself while falling asleep.

Incubation - *Sleep*
This is the time for the consciously gathered information and material to sink into the subconscious mind. There it is "played with" by the metaphoric, unassuming, ambiguous, uninhibited, synthesizing, potential projecting, intuitive faculties of the subconscious. Now thesis, (consideration of similarities); antithesis, (consideration of differences); and synthesis, (consideration of combinations and compromises) take place.

Creative Idea - *Dream*
The inspiration, new approach, insight etc., may be a full blown creation or a seed for further development. In a dream incubation process this will be the dream and its interpretation in relation to the incubation phrase or question.
"Nothing so much convinces me of the boundlessness of the human mind as its operation in dreaming." - Chulow

Follow-up - *Dream Journal Record*
Recording the idea and performing the action are needed to bring the creative product into manifestation. A certain amount of trust in the intuitive faculty is required.

When you first begin dream incubating, especially if you haven't been monitoring your dreams in a dream journal, it may take some time to train the dream mind. But, be patient. Research shows that people who practice to develop this skill get guidance eight out of ten times within three nights of starting an incubation. Get a dream journal and start mining the gold of your dreams. You will discover other treasures also.

According to Jeve Moorman, "*Status quo* is Latin for 'the mess we're in.'" Practical creative changes are always needed, why don't you dream up some of them?

I'd like to leave you with the thought expressed by Fredrick Kekule to a scientific convention when discussing his dream-based Nobel Prize in Chemistry:

"Let us learn to dream, gentlemen,
then perhaps we shall discover the truth."

*"What you can do or dream you can, begin it;
boldness has genius, power and magic in it."*
- Goethe

Byron W. Boothe
Byron Boothe & Associates, Inc.
P.O. Box 47128
Wichita, KS 67201
(316) 263-1166

Byron W. Boothe

Byron W. Boothe is an Entrepreneur. His broad experience includes all levels of business, from owning retail stores, to active investing in wholesale and manufacturing firms, founding two nation-wide franchise companies, and corporate level operations and management. Boothe was also the founder and President of Boothe Advertising Agency, Inc., which served many national accounts including Rexall Drug.

As President of Byron Boothe & Associates, Inc., a business consulting firm, he is a much sought-after consultant and popular speaker on marketing and future trends. Byron is also a seminar leader and producer, publisher of a financial newsletter, and author.

He has been involved in franchising on a national basis for over twenty years and in 1985 Boothe was selected as one of Entrepreneur Magazine's twenty-five "Entrepreneur of the Year" recipients.

Byron is currently a nationwide specialist in marketing insurance programs and a member of the National Association of Life Underwriters. He concentrates on making insurance an asset for individuals, companies and non-profit organizations.

He is a member of the International Business Brokers Association and a designated BCB — Board Certified Broker. Byron is also a member of the Institute of Business Appraisers and the Institute of Certified Business Counselors. He carries a wealth of knowledge applicable to survival in any business environment.

Most importantly, Byron has an active interest in seeing other people achieve their dreams. He is a believer in success.

Responsible Innovation

By Byron W. Boothe

*"Man's mind, once stretched by a new idea,
never regains its original dimensions."*
                                    - Oliver Wendell Holmes

The Museum of Innovation Has-Beens

The handwritten sign on the telephone pole reads,
GARAGE SALE, 937 Litchfield. I can't control myself
— I have to stop! A casual "snoop" through a really
good garage sale can be reckoned to a trip through the

"museum of has-been innovations." I can't help but feel sorry for the 8mm movie camera that is still in the box; it looks brand new. You can tell that it has been part of a loving and caring family. The asking price is only $5.00 for this piece of their family history. But what am I going to do with it? It definitely is not in the antique category, but maybe if I hold on to it my heirs can cash in when the 8mm becomes "the collectible" in 2080. Who knows? Who predicts the collectible craze?

I know everyone cringes when they think about the times their parents brought out the 8mm movie projectors and aimed it towards the sheet on the wall demonstrating to anyone who was willing to watch, what a talented family they had...look, they can ski and fall down...blow out birthday candles...what talent!

What an innovation the 8mm movie camera proved to be for people everywhere; but now it is a "has been" relegated to garage sales and garbage cans. It cannot even begin to complete with the video products that have become the innovations of the 80's.

My, How You've Changed!

Often times we think of change in terms of "things." When we think of innovation, the space shuttle, the computer in your car and the microwave come to mind. But the 60's brought with it "the change of the human being." Millions of people read *I'm Okay, You're Okay* and determined that they were in fact the most important person in the world and began to act accordingly. Divorce was rampant and what a boost it was for the American economy. Every time a family would split, it would necessitate setting up another residence, buying another car, another toaster — not to mention the tremendous legal fees.

Is change always positive? When I hear, "let's change that, let's make some changes," in my mind we are going to make things better. But I have learned that change should be made very carefully and with much regard to what that change will bring. You must constantly be aware that if you do not take charge of change, it will soon take charge of you. You must be willing to be the master of the change you create.

We are losing our ozone layer, thanks to change... thanks to innovation. Do you think an innovative person can discover a way to reproduce or repair one of God's creations? Do you think man can reproduce "Old Faithful" in Yellowstone Park after being partially destroyed by a fire — a fire that man, the great innovator, could not contain?

Who Is This Guy, Byron Boothe?

By now, you are thinking, "Who is this guy, Byron Boothe? Why is he included in the book of great innovators?" I want you to know that I *am* an innovator. I will be an innovator until I die and then my innovations will be carried out by my six children and all the other friends and associates that I have developed through the years. I tell these horror stories because I want all of these people to be responsible innovators.

I want them to create things that will have a lifespan of over five minutes. (What are all the carpet cleaners going to do when every household has stain resistant carpet? What will video rental stores do when you can "dial up" your video request via the telephone?) I want them to discover ways to enhance our ecological situation, not destroy it. I want them to concentrate on positive change for the human race and preserving the natural resources that were given to us by God. Do we really think He will create another world for us to destroy with our innovations? I think not.

Look around the room that you are occupying right now. What do you need in that room to survive for one week? Do you need your word processor, your VCR, your dictating equipment, the fax machine, the copy machine? Do you, at this very moment, have access to food and water?

My point being, that most of the attention has been given to objects that make our life physically easier. Are the innovators giving any attention to "peace of mind"? Do any of these things give you peace of mind at night? Can your fax machine give you a hug and tell you everything will be better in the morning? Are your fondest memories of the night you and your word processor created a beautiful story, or do they involve another human being?

Find a Want and Fill It

Let me share some of the innovations I had a part in developing during my lifetime. I think you will see that the majority of the innovations were designed to have an on-going lifespan and they all have one thing in common...I found a want and filled it. People act on wants more than on needs.

Furniture and appliance rental: This service will be around forever. There will always be people, unfortunately, who cannot afford to pay cash for these items or obtain the credit to purchase them through a bank, etc. However, all people "want" nice furniture. People will continue to move and a great majority of those people have no desire to own furniture, so they rent. Twenty years ago, if you were in either of these situations, you would not have had this opportunity and/or choice available to you.

Franchises: Although this was not my concept, I have been involved in the implementation of this structure. During past years, I owned a company that had 2000 franchised drug stores and another company that sold 300 franchises in the video industry in just two years.

Facsimile: I assisted in the research and development phase of a company which utilizes facsimile machines and taxi cabs to deliver documents anywhere in the United States within three hours and I still serve on their Board of Directors. This small but growing company has been able to deliver a service where even giant Federal Express failed.

Services: This is an area that will continue to grow in the 80's and 90's. I have assisted many clients in the strategic planning of their organizations, being a "trend watcher" and providing my clients with an edge in many different areas. Two of my clients in particular have specialized, one in fire and demolition repair and the other in personal services for executive men and women, which does everything from planning your office Christmas party to standing in line for your car tags. Their businesses are booming and will continue to grow. Again, this is a concept with a long lifespan. A computer cannot replace these services.

Associated Druggists: This business still lives on and will as long as the entrepreneurial spirit is alive and well. I developed a system that allowed independent drug store owners to compete with the mega-corporation chain pharmacies.

My greatest innovations have been in identifying better ways to maximize, use and position things, companies and, most of all, people. I am extremely proud of my family and all of the people that I have helped direct, reward and reach for the stars.

Innovators...
Listen, Look, and Assimilate

Innovation for me is a full-time, on-going process. I surround myself with intelligent people. (And it does not bother me one bit if all of them are smarter than I. Listening and observing are easy and cheap— and the best form of education, in my opinion.) I gather ideas from printed media to the tune of reading four newspapers on a daily basis; also, with the help of an information specialist, I read 75 magazines and 120 newsletters every month. In my spare time, I read and I read. My personal goal is to read a minimum of 70 books every year.

This on-going education has made me a professional in predicting the trends. You can bet that every so-called genius has a resource library that they utilize. Every good songwriter or poet is bound to have a well-used Thesaurus and every innovative person is going to have a wealth of information at his finger tips.

An idea is a culmination of experiences that a

person has had, combined with the knowledge that he has acquired. If you want the ideas to continue to flow, you must continue to read, to listen, and to observe. You must continue to record all of the innovations that you devise. Consider using a Rolodex to store your ideas. Keep it on your desk, and the minute a good concept comes to mind, write it down. You can worry about expanding on the idea later. Education gives you power; I will take power over money any day. People can take your money away from you, but they cannot take your education. Education cannot be repossessed.

I have found the following books always provide inspiration for me: *Think and Grow Rich* by Napoleon Hill; *Psycho-cybernetics* by Maxwell Maltz; *Scientific Advertising* by Claude Hopkins, and my number one inspirational book, the Bible.

I've Never Had a Creative Thought in My Life!

I hear many of the people who attend my seminars say, "but I am just not creative." I often ask them if they visualize themselves as poor people. If they do see themselves as poor people, they probably are not capable of innovation and they will never be capable of innovation. After all, how many poor people do you know that could be categorized as innovative? Now keep in mind that when I speak of riches, I am speaking of "riches of the mind" and not the pocketbook.

The Richest Woman I Will Ever Know

My grandmother, (I am sure the bankers would have classified her as a poor woman), was the richest woman I have known to date. She was blessed with the ability to change the unfortunate situation into a fortunate situation. During the depression, when people did not have enough to eat, she managed to create a meal out of most anything that fed an endless number of people in need.

The atmosphere that evolved was not one of a "soup kitchen," but one of mutual love and respect—a gathering of friends, even though most of the people were strangers. I never saw her turn anybody away. Grandma Berry took the little that she had and turned it into what appeared to be an abundant food supply. That was sheer innovation. It was her mind set. In her mind she was not a poor person; she was a blessed person and what she had she would share. Didn't Jesus try to teach that concept to His followers?

Being Poor is a Permanent State of Mind, Being Broke is Only Temporary

If you are poor in your mind, if you are not thankful for the powerful mind that you are blessed with, innovation will not come your way. I hear people say that they are not creative and I always wonder who told them they were not creative. Was it their mother or father? Was it their first grade teacher? You must understand that we are all creative people — some of you have simply not used this ability.

YOU NEED TO INVENTORY YOUR LIFE-STYLE AND SEE IF THERE IS A REASON THAT YOUR INNOVATIVE JUICES ARE NOT ALLOWED TO FLOW.

Ask yourself the following questions:

1. What is the high point of your day?
2. Do you look forward to going home at night? Do you have a favorite spot in your home?
3. Do you have a partner/spouse who supports you and is interested in your day to day world?
4. How are new ideas received in your business and/or home life?
5. Are there any people in your life who tend to "zap" your positive energy flow?
6. Are you afraid of failure?
7. Is money the only reason that you work? If

you had an abundant amount of money, would you continue to work?

8. Do you have a creative talent that you have not utilized in a longtime (playing the piano, painting a picture, etc.)?

9. Do you hear the word "no" a lot?

10. If you present an idea, do people say... that's stupid or someone else has already thought of that... or we tried that before and it didn't work?

11. Are people rewarded for innovative behavior in your place of business?

12. Are you in a financial position that makes it difficult to vary from the norm? Does your partner/spouse expect you to make a certain amount of money each and every month?

13. Would your partner/spouse be willing to lower their standard of living in order for your innovation to become a reality?

Don't Just Stand There...Do Something!!

Once you have completed this inventory, let me give you the very best piece of advice I can give you about being innovative. If you have an idea, **write it down.** Periodically, I will go through my "light bulb" files and pull out all the great ideas I have had over the years...and you know what I generally discover? Someone else has acted on my great idea. If you have a great idea, DO something. Make a decision. Go for it! Do the homework and background research necessary to determine if this is a viable project. Seek out the advice of people who have a worthwhile opinion to contribute and utilize the thoughts of specialists in their areas. You will find that most people are more than willing to share their expertise with you. Do not let all of your decisions be influenced by your next door neighbor or your brother-in-law or your hair dresser. Always keep in mind that your opinion is usually the best one, if you really believe in it.

You might be thinking, "If I discuss my new-found innovation with all of these people, somebody is going to steal my idea and take the ball and run with it, before I can get to the patent office." But innovation theft rarely happens. Do not hesitate to have your idea or process patented. This is a legal process that I utilize and I have never regretted the money that I have expended.

The most common excuse for lack of innovation is, "I don't have the money!" What a lousy excuse! If you believe in the concept, you can find the money. Trust me, you can do it! There is always more money chasing ideas than there are people who take the time to develop the ideas. I have found that true innovative ideas are not a dime a dozen. Contrary to that, I found hundreds of "lazy people" with a gem of an idea who are too lazy to implement the idea.

Take What You've Got
and Do Something With It!

My hope is, in the future, people will be obliged to accept the responsibility for their innovations. My dream is to see the American public take what they've got and do something with it. What is going to happen to this nation if we continue to be a nation that creates slums?

We suffer from "keeping up with the Jones" syndrome. Nothing ever quite meets our expectations. We always want a better house, a better car, a better office. This year when I moved my office, I opted to buy an old warehouse and renovate it. I would venture to say that if I had not made this decision my community would have been burdened with another deserted warehouse.

You cannot believe the interest that my buying decision has aroused, and I predict I will be the pacesetter in renovation in this area. A good innovator is not afraid to be the first in line and there is no bigger thrill when the masses begin to line up behind you.

Remember, innovation is God's way
of short circuiting status quo.

"Creativity can solve any problem.
The creative act, the defeat of habit by originality,
overcomes everything."
- George Lois

Ernest L. Weckbaugh
Casa Graphics, Inc.
1718 Rogers Place, Suite 1A
Burbank, CA 91504
818 842-4AR

Ernest L. Weckbaugh

Ernest L. Weckbaugh is president of Casa Graphics, Inc. (since 1976) and has been a graphic designer, illustrator, cartoonist, calligrapher, teacher, publisher and writer since 1948. As a past president in Toastmasters International, he has won his club's Toastmaster of the Year award five times, plus numerous area-wide humorous speech contests. He earned a bachelor of arts degree with high honor from California State University at Los Angeles (Alpha Gamma Sigma and Phi Kappa Phi Honor Societies) with additional studies at Occidental College and at the Art Center College of Design.

His working experience actually began in 1937 as a child actor in the "Our Gang" comedies, under contract to Warner Bros. Studios. He enlisted for four years in the Air Force during the Korean War, where he was assigned to Special Services as an illustrator. He and his wife Patty have been guest lecturers at UCLA since 1982 in the entrepreneurial program, speaking on self-marketing and on their experiences building a creative small business.

As a calligrapher, he has done the Humanitarian Awards for the National Conference of Christians and Jews, the Grammy Awards for the National Association of Recording Arts and Sciences, the Golden Globe Awards for the Hollywood Foreign Press Association among many others for over twenty-five years. He has taught courses in calligraphy at Disney Studios, the Glendale Unified School District and at a number of art seminars in recent years.

Mr. Weckbaugh has written and illustrated a series of four books for Christian youth, published by Standard Publishing of Cincinnati, Ohio, plus numerous newspaper and magazine articles on a variety of subjects.

Don't Neglect Your "Child"

By Ernest L. Weckbaugh

*"In the creative process there is the father,
the author of the play; the mother, the actor pregnant
with the part; and the child, the role to be born."*
- Konstantin Stanislavski, "An Actor Prepares"

When I see young people staring into space, doodling intently, muttering or talking to themselves, I can recognize kindred spirits. Any member of my family will tell you that most of the time as a youth my mind was "absent." I would sit for hours in the top of the peach tree and stare off into the sky. I was known for locking myself into the only bathroom of our tiny house for hours to study the dictionary. Of all the books in the house, this was my favorite. It never told me what to see or feel like other books did. With one word as a starting point, I could create my own stories and fantasies. Each new word unlocked a new chamber of my private world. While the rest of the family took turns pounding on the bathroom door, I trained myself to ignore such distractions, and it was there that I learned the valuable art of concentration. To this day my brother and sister can't understand how I come up with ideas. I'm sure they think it's like trying to draw water from an empty well.

I used to fill every blank sheet of paper that I could find from top to bottom with little drawings. While walking home alone from school, I would carry on a two-sided, animated conversation...out loud. I recently found a book entitled, "What to Say When You Talk to Yourself" by Shad Helmstetter, and I finally realized that I was not alone in having my own little world.

I was always making something. Before I could even pronounce the word, I would announce to everyone in my family that I was working on an "im-ben-shun." I had a clear vision of each little project and I pursued every one of them relentlessly. You must realize that all of this weirdness gave my mother a great deal of concern. So much so that when I did succeed in earning a living as an artist, she never could believe there was any future in it for me. I realize now that all of this twisted behavior was simply the early signs of a creative mind. Some people express themselves socially, others athletically...this was the only way I had, being naturally shy and uncoordinated.

I'm convinced the roots of our creativity reach far down into our childhood and that a combination of circumstances and natural tendencies seem to conspire, causing us to take that direction. I recall a number of events that occured when I was young that contributed directly to the creative warping of my mind.

A Noisy Reunion

Most people have a colorful relative or two. I had them by the carloads. Relatives from both sides of our family had a habit of dropping in on us from Colorado, Nebraska, and even Panama. I loved the excitement when they came and all the funny stories that were passed around, the presents and the silver dollars my brother, sister and I always received. However, I noticed my mother wasn't often very happy about their arrival. With worrying about the necessary meals and how to squeeze everyone into three small bedrooms, she picked up my habit of frequently talking to herself.

The fun ended for me when bedtime came. Relatives were assigned several to a room, but the children were sent there first. I listened from my room to the frequent outbursts of laughter for an hour or so, followed by the movement and hushed voices in the hall as they prepared to retire. The three assigned to my room shuffled in, quietly apologizing, smelling of cigars and beer, whispering goodnight, knocking over furniture in the dark and sincerely hoping they had not awakened me. I had been spending the previous hour in the dark straining to hear the forbidden stories they had saved for our absence. My excitement had not yet turned to exhaustion, and the novelty of these large adults playing "Three Stooges" with the unseen furniture ended any thoughts of sleep.

However, they had no problem falling asleep...soundly. Suddenly, I was startled, upright, wide-awake and terrified by their deafening outbursts. I realized I was faced with a long-playing chorus of snoring without any hope of sleep for the next seven hours. It was going to be a test of my sanity to rival any sadistic horror movie, and somehow I had to "think" my way through it.

The Bombs Bursting In Air

I slowly drifted off, not into sleep, but into a fantasy. It was the summer of 1942 and America had just entered World War II. With my pillow as my parachute and backrest, I sat at the controls of my fully-loaded B-24 bomber, somewhere in the night sky over Germany. As I pulled on my toy goggles, I realized at that very moment I was surrounded by Germans (these were my father's relatives). But...they also happened to be loyal Americans, and I was counting on them that night. On my left, at 10 o'clock high,

Uncle Eugene illuminated the darkness with his nasal artillery. I had little to fear, though, with the steady drone of my Pratt & Whitney engines to reassure me. It was really Uncle Ed and Aunt Lydia, but a more faithful drone you couldn't wish for. It seemed an eternity (these missions always took longer than you anticipated), but the constant hum of the rest of the squadron (in the adjoining bedrooms) gave me comfort and encouragement. At last we reached our target area. Rapidly we prepared the bombs for release. At the precise moment, right on cue, Aunt Lydia switched to a whistling sound. I knew that I could count on her. Thirty thousand feet below I began to hear the blockbusters exploding on target. I almost cheered out loud!

By the Dawn's Early Light

I wasn't worried about the long flight home. Our giant engines still pulsed away with only an occasional cough, sputter or wheeze. I can still remember the faint light on the horizon through the windows. We landed at dawn. I felt strangely victorious at breakfast that morning. I had survived the night without losing my mind and I'd had an exciting and memorable adventure. In the years that followed, my imagination came to my rescue on many occasions. I began to believe that I could do, or be, whatever I wished through the magic of creativity.

Up, Up and Away

However, when I joined the Air Force, the military establishment provided a strong challenge to that kind of thinking. Immediately, my rights resided in the minds and plans of sergeants and captains more firmly than they ever had with any civilian employer and with fewer options (for example, they wouldn't let me quit). But I discovered that there was another side to that immovable obstacle, just like anything else. I found great satisfaction in creating the illusion of freedom during my off-duty time.

Weekends were special times of escape for many of us. Painting the local scene with a fellow G.I. put me instantly on the other side of the world from the bureaucracies and personalities of the Air Force. Fred was a few years older than I was and a gifted artist, having attended The Art Students' League in New York. He was an able teacher as well as craftsman, often opening my eyes to unseen beauty. The glee of running away from authority and doing the "unexpected" was a trip back to my childhood.

Tennessee on the Tundra

A swampy expanse of land to the east of the city of Anchorage, Alaska, stretched to the base of the nearby foothills behind which rose the cloud-capped Chugach Mountains. Centered in this wild, magnificent vista was the humblest, tumbledown shack I'd ever seen outside of a movie. Repelled and saddened by such poverty, I turned to my street-wise friend for his reaction. His enthusiasm made me take a second look. He pointed out the textures of the decaying wood, its roughness against the creamy snow of Mt. Susitna. A stillwater pool in the foreground created a mirror image. The roof's sharp angles were silhouetted against the soft, rolling hills. He focused my imagination on the full spectrum of colors within each rotting plank.

But then, in the narrow doorway of this bucolic bungalow there appeared the slim figure of a girl. Her black skin, the plain cotton dress, her way of standing...it was pure Tennessee Williams.

My friend's point of view and the creative insights he revealed to me opened my perceptions to nearly a fourth dimension. It has given me the desire over the years, perhaps even the power, to see beyond the obvious and a reluctance to settle for one or two possibilities if, in fact, there may be dozens.

The Impressionists

With my seeing-eye friend Fred, I began a creative odyssey into downtown and backwoods Alaska. The colors and contrasts, the new crowding out the old, the hurried growth of the city...it all reminded us of the impressionists' rapid style of painting with bright, raw colors. Where I would see only a gray and somber church, Fred could visualize a future moment when the congregation, in full and colorful dress, would be descending the steps bathed in the rays of the mid-morning sun. We would have to be set up and ready, however, so that on Sunday, with the building and the sky freshly brushed on each canvas, we would be able to capture the moment in a ten-minute burst of energy after the doors opened. A little touch up here and there, after the crowd left, gave us each a prize worthy of a young Van Gogh or Renoir.

Innovation can often be an accident. One can only hope for it and then be able to recognize it. This happened to us one Sunday morning while we were painting on the main street of Anchorage. The gaudy signs lining both sides of the street had fascinated us with their colors and jumbled patterns and, being pseudo-impressionists, we decided one day to paint it. Toulouse-Lautrec would have loved the scene. What happened next was an experience I'll never forget. As we were absorbed in our rendering of each overlapping neon sign, we failed to notice how dark it was getting. We did notice a certain grittiness in the texture of our paint, however. As we finally looked up we realized what was happening. A volcanic eruption hundreds of miles south of Anchorage was overshadowing the city with its cloud of dust. The dust was impregnating the wet surface of our finished paintings, and it was creating a unique facsimile of the scene before us. The thick white dust created a monumental mess for everyone else, but it turned my humble work of art into a rare treasure.

Drawing From "Real Life"

The two partners in an advertising agency in Anchorage opened their doors to us and welcomed us as equals. Always eager to balance my military lifestyle with some local culture, our paths had crossed many times during different community activities held by the civilian population, and we had become friends. Local bars were turned overnight into art galleries for a week or two. Any room large enough to hold fifty or more people and a piano became a rehearsal hall for a community chorus or a musical play in a city eager for both physical and cultural growth.

One evening at chorus rehearsal, my friends said that what we really needed was a life drawing class. We could hold it in the spacious production room of their agency. A model had been found and they were looking for a large enough group to share her fee and make it affordable. Well, needless to say, life drawing had always been one of my happiest "real life" experiences (the term we used for our non-military past). I had been drawing since my early childhood, but when I attended my first "life" class with a live model, I knew instantly that an art career was the right choice for me. So I eagerly spread the word among those I felt might be artistically interested. The only criteria was to have drawing skills and agree to leave the sketches at the agency. Somehow we felt that our barracks' buddies might not understand our true intentions.

Our first meeting was very well attended. Our model had come early and was changing in an adjoining room as we arrived. She finally appeared, demurely attired in a robe, and she introduced herself as the wife of a soldier at nearby Fort Richardson. As she then assumed her position atop the stool in the center of the room and dropped her robe, it was easy to read the minds of the rest of those in the room. Does her husband know? Does he think she's waiting tables once a week at a downtown diner? Is he going to appear at the door some night in an ugly mood? How skilled is he in the use of automatic weapons?

But she was obviously a skilled and experienced model, and our misgivings faded as, week after week, we maintained perfect attendance. About the time that this weekly habit had become completely addictive, our second worst fear was realized. Her husband's tour of duty was over. After she left, we tried taking turns as "the model" (with our clothes on, of course), but it just wasn't the same. She proved to be irreplacable and it wasn't because we all didn't try to find someone. With this experience I learned that all good things must end. It left me with the feeling that, as good as things may seem to be, the best is often temporary. However, I have the power of my imagination to continually try to make things better. This is why I believe truly successful, creative people

are constantly looking ahead, never assuming anything, never completely at rest.

The "Water" Colorist

On one weekend morning in summer, part of our
former life-drawing group set out to paint the mud
flats of Anchorage. The tidewaters of Prince William
Sound rose and fell about 35 feet every day, creating
a sprawling mud flat where only a few hours before
there had been a beautiful, boat-filled lagoon. We
agreed to spend the day painting in watercolor the
different views from the deck of one of the stranded
boats, stuck at odd angles here and there in the brown
ooze. Boats and planes had fascinated me since I was
a boy, and so had the idea of being someplace I
shouldn't be.

We boarded one of the nearby boats by building a
crude wooden bridge from a pile of abandoned boxes
and two-by-fours. This spanned the mud and allowed
us to carefully hand our supplies and equipment from
person to person. The boat, in spite of its slanting
deck, looked fairly stable and was about 20 feet from
the dock. Then each of the four of us settled down on
board to paint the view of our choice.

Shortly after we had set up, we were cordially
greeted by a very large and friendly shaggy dog, who
had somehow negotiated the wobbly gangplank. He
nuzzled everyone amiably, then quietly curled up on
the bow of the boat and fell asleep.

Several hours passed before our artistic concentration was broken by hunger and other fundamental needs. Until that moment, no one had noticed that the quietly rising tide was now about chest deep all around the boat. We were soon to be afloat and, worst of all, our bridge was underwater. We quickly organized ourselves and, like a well-rehearsed team, began the tiptoed transporting of our precious gallery of paintings from ship to shore. No one wanted to test the bottom mud, so great pains were taken to keep us and our equipment as high and dry as possible. Our shoes were soaked, but everyone made it without falling in. We proudly displayed our creations in a semi-circle on the dock, propping them up on the railing and on our equipment boxes. Then we stepped back for a critical appraisal.

The dog must have been observing our departure and he decided to join us. Our back was to the boat as we concentrated in mutual admiration on our paintings. Forgetting about the bridge this time, he just jumped in and swam across. Soaked with water, he scrambled up onto the dock to join our little circle of art critics. The first time any of us realized he was there was when he moved to the center of our circle of paintings and planted his four feet wide apart.

Our facial expressions indicated that all of us knew what was coming. Our reaction time, however, was too slow. Before we could even blink, the entire dock area, everything and everyone, was saturated. The blinding force and sheer quantity of water from his shaking fur stunned us. Apprehensive examination revealed our worst fears; he had successfully erased our entire day's output. Unconcerned and still dripping, he hopped from one to another of us for attention and approval. And why not? He was certainly the fastest and most prolific "water" colorist in the group. Our anger and shock quickly turned to hysterical laughter when one of us suggested the dog probably possessed the soul of an art critic from a past life.

With a flip of his tail, that shaggy mutt had destroyed our illusions and brought us, with a splash, back down to earth. No one knew it then, but that was to be a common occurence during the rest of our lives. But if creative types are to survive, they need to learn to be resilient. They must develop a toughness and tenacity. Then, in time, they'll eventually prove the worth of their ideas and talent.

In the Bible, in I Corinthians 13:11, the apostle Paul said, "When I was a child, I talked like a child, I thought like a child, I reasoned like a child. When I became a man, I put away childish things." I think we can assume that Paul probably had a normal childhood, a satisfying relationship with his friends, and two loving parents. Whereas my own eccentric youth, like many others, was marred by the stigma of divorce, plus the pressure of performing in films (the "Our Gang" comedies, etc.) while constantly being taken away from school. Add to that the trauma of World War II, with all the moving from city to city for the "war effort," and you get a picture of lost childhood.

I spent years with an empty feeling, mourning and resenting what had been taken from me. Then I began to realize that it could all be regained by working with children. In the process of creating puzzles and games, with the necessary teaching and testing of ideas with young people, I didn't have to "put away childish things." I could be that child again. But this time I could add the perspective of maturity, the assurance of experience, and the self-esteem gained through years of trial and success. This time I could have friends and excitement and be free of the pressure and anxiety I can so clearly remember.

And this time, the person who is enjoying these new experiences, with the loving support of friends and family to share them is the child I am...and never was.

"The human race is governed by its imagination."
- Napoleon Bonaparte

"Rmnas" Ruthmarie Arguello-Sheehan
Story Arts Projects
1471 Chanticleer Avenue
Santa Cruz,CA 95062
408 475-8939, 714 830-4149

Ruthmarie Arguello-Sheehan

The excitement of living each day to its fullest seems to be the theme of this bouncy international Storyteller artist, educator and motivational speaker. Spiritual growth, new-age ideas, and exploring the possibilities of every person reaching his or her ultimate experience intrigues her imagination.

A lifetime Storyteller, she was one of the first in modern U.S. to be honored for the past forty years as "a master, professional Storyteller Artist," by the thousands who have heard her.

Former founder-director of The American Storytelling Resource Center, Inc., a highly respected international Storytelling organization for folk, educational and motivational Storytellers, Ruthmarie recently resigned from also organizing its annual festivals and conferences, "To return, to full-time Storytelling and spiritual growth, and to sharing all my adventures to inspire others."

Invited to perform, teach and collect stories all over the world, she has been honored in Europe, the Middle East, Africa, and China and shares her unique and exciting experiences and stories with her audiences now in the U.S.

One of the few Storytellers to custom-produce programs, she has woven her stories to assist all kinds of social equality issues, such as handicapped persons, women, children, and environmental projects, but has been welcomed equally in corporate, business or political arenas.

A lover of the outdoors, her TV programs frequently told stories of the mysteries of nature to wide family audiences. Her sense of humor is always on the edge of laughter and playfulness and lights up her programs. Her award-winning video tapes and audio cassettes are popular with adults as well as children. She is author of numerous stories, articles and educational handbooks, and is a certified Tai Chi Chih teacher.

For the past six years she has worked as a Leisure Services and Recreation Director, emphasizing the importance of continued learning and playing for the growing-older adult population.

Ruthmarie believes a Storyteller should be included in the next space flight in order to absorb and interpret the experience interestingly. She may apply! Our "Storyteller in Space" or on earth is a fascinating speaker.

Re-Creation
Through the Art of Storytelling

By Ruthmarie Arguello-Sheehan

"The Tale is told over and over again in the brain, and flows through the body and spirit for nourishment, until One Holy Instant it is finally completely unified, and WE ARE THE STORY!"

- Rmnas

From the Ending Comes the Beginning!

"What's the sense of our coming to these old people's rest homes," complained one of my college students from my Storytelling class. "They just seem to fall asleep and don't hear us!"

The student's complaint seemed valid. Early every Friday evening several students and I visited these homes to play our guitars, sing and tell stories. Mostly the old people did seem to nod, smile absently, or go to sleep.

I asked myself how much longer I could dangle extra class credits, and keep the students coming for this community service project, when they didn't feel appreciated. I prayed for a sign to continue what my Intuition knew for the Truth.

That very evening I was telling a funny Irish Folktale and to my dismay I suddenly forgot the usual ending! It had never happened to me before. I hope it never does again. Being a writer now proved to be an added advantage and I was able quickly to create a new ending.

My students smiled for they knew my usual ending, but the old folks seemed to nod on.

I had always insisted we greet and say "goodbye" to each individual before we left. "Touch gently these fragile spirits with your hands, but touch powerfully with your personal love of verbal communication," I had urged each student. So, I led the farewell line myself.

The first person in the half-circle was a tiny, white-haired, very old lady with her chin dropped down on her chest throughout most of the performances.

I touched her frail hand and said, "Did you enjoy our music and stories?"

She lifted her trembling chin. She looked directly into my eyes with her clear eyes, the bluest I've ever seen, and faintly smiled as she said, "I liked *your* made-up ending better, honey, than the old one! Thank you, I haven't heard it in years!"

My students heard it, too. Nothing more had to be said about returning on Friday nights for the rest of the semester. We ALL wanted to continue NOW!

The seemingly obvious exterior, I have frequently found, does not reflect the power of a Story to enter the memory, the subconscious, and superconscious of a listener.

The personal power of Storytelling reaches beyond external barriers of sophistication, age, sex, ethnics, culture or even language, when done with deep loving intentions and choices for the recipients.

> *"He who knows others is wise.*
> *He who knows himself is enlightened."*
>   - Unknown

Knowing your own motives for using the art of Storytelling has always seemed to be most important to me.

It is an Art that does not feed definite images like TV, that the listener *must* accept as a spectator. It allows each individual to hear and assimilate as much as the listener is able, ready and willing to self-picture at that particular moment. The listener can recall the moment whenever he wants to do so.

Overcoming All Fears

God has not given us a spirit of fear,
but of power, and of love and of a sound mind.
- 2 Timothy1:7

"There is a death contract on your life," a young
Iranian stage technician whispered to me backstage
in 1976 when I was invited to perform before thousands at the beautiful palace amphitheater for ten
nights.

I had noticed how closely my husband, young son
and I had been taken care of by the Shah's wife's representatives, and the Institute for Children and
Young Adults Educational and Art Enrichment.
During all of our weeks of travel and my performances, we had been tended with generosity and care.

My performance at this international festival as
the only invited United States representative of the
performing arts, caused me to feel a serious responsibility.

For two years I had negotiated with Middle Eastern representatives to make these arrangements. I
actually wrote the final shows combining puppetry,
music, and oral Storytelling while in the area. I had
designed and created special costumes, puppets,
stages and music very carefully before leaving the
United States. I paid careful attention to adjustment
of actual words and idiosyncrasies of customs when
actually in each country. I did not want ever to offend

anyone's religious or cultural customs, so I had studied and prepared before leaving. Yet, there were always last minute changes. "On-the-spot knowledge and intuition," I called it.

My philosophy is, *"the amount of attention paid to detail is what makes a professional."*

I had made several changes before opening night. Why would anyone want to kill me? I was here to entertain and to communicate pleasure and mutual communication through my arts. It was not a political show, but I had discovered we are *all* involved in politics by the very fact we are public or civic creatures.

My opening night was July 4th, a fun-filled, bicentennial celebration night at home. Perhaps it would be a symbol to rebels here to harm a representative of the United States on such a date. After all, many proclamations of honor had been written to me personally, as well as in the press, about the one-of-a-kind invitation.

Especially unique was the fact that I was a woman Storyteller, even though I had performed all over the world. Women were just beginning to realize some freedom in this country. My appearances were unusual, as women Storytellers had only performed in private here. Men Storytellers at tea houses were a common event.

I was assured that we would be protected. Soldiers were quite apparent, as I looked out from the stage wings. The temperature was over 100 degrees even as the sun began to set and the audience was crowding in with many more adults even than children.

I knew I would be blinded by the stage lights and TV recording lights throughout most of the one-and-a-half hour non-stop show. My Iranian sound, light and stage crew were all ready after days of rehearsing and remarkably few language barriers. Somehow, even in China, Europe, Africa or the Middle East, I have never had a language barrier.

My husband and son agreed that I should make the decision myself as to whether to go on or not. They would help with some of the behind-the-stage puppets, but I was the one out there as a potential target.

I prayed for guidance. Quietly in my dressing-room tent I finally relaxed and the thought came again: *Let go and let God!* I had checked out all I could control. The rest was up to God. I heard my opening music. I went out on that stage unafraid.

Half-way through the show I approached the edge of the stage. I bent my right knee down, holding a huge, funny stork puppet, and through my ventriloquism, we both sang. I could sense my audience's delight and was just beginning to back up when I saw a dark shadow, pointing something square and black at me, run to the edge of the stage pit.

Instantly I knew I could not run away in time if this was a bomb or a gun. The music played merrily.

"Thy will be done. Thy will be done!" was all I could think, as I backed to center stage trying not to trip over my long costume. I could not see my audience. I had to imagine them there, but I did see soldiers rush forward and drag the dark shadow of a person away.

It was a miracle, I realized later, that I had not been startled enough to fall over the edge of the stage.

At the time, I simply continued my show. My years of having my own TV show had trained my "four-part mind" as I call it: (1) the part that actually says the words and moves my body; (2) the part that observes my performance outside of me and helps make corrections; (3) the part that watches the director and other crews for instructions for time, cameras, technical needs, etc.; and (4) the intuition sensitivity to the reactions of a live audience or imagined TV audience.

It is this fourth part of the mind that is most important. It is this total discipline that kept me going under unexpected interruptions. It was my Faith-in-God Power directing my life, when I asked for it, that carried on that opening-night show in Tehran, Iran.

After the show, my advisors told me it had been an Egyptian news photographer who had pointed an old light meter at me and they had dragged him off for questioning! Whatever the explanation, I knew it was another demonstration of creative innovation through instant faith.

Courage is only an afterthought, I know, to an inner faith based on love of self and thus of others. The Trilogy is always evident in the "me," "you" and "we," especially in performing such an intimate art as Storytelling.

Seeing the Invisible

" Trust! Greatness will come out of you.
There is no smallness in life, only taking
small parts.
You are the chooser.
Our Provider always lets us decide. "
- Rmnas

The temperature was minus forty. The wind howled around the large one-room schoolhouse outside the Eskimo village that lay miles from any other on the Bering Sea tundra.

I felt tired at that moment as I sat next to the big oil stove waiting for the entire village of 150 people to gather for my first night of Storytelling.

The children all seemed to have runny noses, I noticed, but they were all beautiful with raven dark hair and curious black eyes. They were constantly feeling my body and pulling my blonde, curly hair. Such a woman they had only seen in occasional movies which had been flown in. This was still a rare subsistence-living village with no TV and only short-wave radio or bush-plane connections to that glittering outside world of modern sophistication.

I realized immediately that my obvious role on this first trip as a Storyteller here was to work with children and adults. How I did it was my own choice. I stayed several weeks in each village, all over tundra Alaska, educating, learning and entertaining through my art.

My most important role, I realized, was to be a "Bridge-between-Cultures." The elders on this first trip spoke Yupik dialect and would not speak English until they trusted me. I had to gain almost instant rapport if I was to accomplish my serious task in the few weeks allotted.

The very fact that I did not look like an Eskimo would have to be an advantage. The educational and cultural arts organization who had arranged this first of its kind trip to these villages, never seen or impossible to visit by most outsiders, had taken a big chance on my knowing intuitively what my role was to be.

They had chosen me, a middle-aged woman Storyteller Artist, mother of five and a grandmother. I was known as an international performer-educator, who never suffered from culture shock, as many younger artists did.

They had been asking me to take this assignment for a couple of years, but I had always been booked ahead. Besides, I didn't want to be in such a cold place, being a seventh generation native of California, and sleeping in down bags on shack floors was starting to lose its appeal. Traveling by bush plane and dog sled held its high adventure, but real dangers, too. This was a unique opportunity for me to prove the "Bridge" theory of a Storyteller being the span between generations.

That first night I knew it had worked, as the old village Shaman identified himself to me and gave me a special gift of a necklace and some of his stories. He said, "I have read your heart. You are Eskimo."

The gift of love given and received had been seen, and told, and acknowledged again.
"From the seed comes the flower
that celebrates
the whisper of Life
in constant renewal of Beauty."
- Rmnas

The Connection Developed by Family Storytelling

I was blessed by coming from several generations of excellent oral Storytellers who grounded me in family stories, as well as techniques of telling.

Young and old, we gathered around the bonfire every long summer night at our Rancho Quito del Dios, high up in the central California coastal mountains of Santa Cruz.

Relatives came and went with their stories of our family, our state's history, bible stories, myths, legends, mysteries, romances, fables, nature stories, fairy tales, ghost stories, and best of all, lots of humor.

"I remember when..." was a great beginning to gather close around the fire and share its warmth and the stories. As children, we were invited to tell stories at an early age. We told stories we had read, as we were encouraged to visit the library and read "everything" we could get our hands on.

At seven years old I had gained a family reputation as the "one who made up stories."

As a quiet, nose-in-the-book, nature loving, fragile child, I came alive in those special sharing times. The older tellers listened attentively, but always critiqued our story organization the next day for us with thoughtful retrospect. It was hard on the ego sometimes, but potent in my training for a lifetime career that I only dreamed of then.

I knew I was really successful when, gathered up in a huge oak tree, my cousin fell out and broke his arm after he got so scared from a ghost story that I told him.

> *"Curiosity is the twinkling of insight*
> *before we decide*
> *to look at the surface of appearance.*
> *Investigation and action*
> *only reaffirm our twinkle*
> *before the Light shines through,*
> *if we desire it."*
>
> - Rmnas

One of the most important lessons of oral Storytelling, I realized at an early age, was that one does not memorize and retell verbatim any stories— but retells stories anew each time. Each story has a life of its own. Each person, of each audience, is a fellow creator with you. You mix the words, such as visual artists do in their paintings, and the creation starts anew each time. The interpretation of each story begins immediately. As the painters choose their colors with careful intent, so must the Storyteller choose words and order.

This art can be like a feast of carefully prepared foods for the imagination and soul. We as Storytellers have a responsibility to use our words with care and intent, and the choice of the best of whatever our particular language has to offer.

We know that creation comes from the inside. The types of stories we retell and images shared reflect much more about who we are than we often realize.

Stories told in our personal, public or job career life should be considered from our inside creation before sharing with others. By the stories we tell we can re-create the attitudes of others about us and change the way we feel about ourselves.

If we have a negative thing happening in our lives we can actively seek out stories that perpetuate opposite, but positive viewpoints, and by forcing ourselves to retell them, we will be amazed at the turn-around in our lives.

> *"By our actions and reactions are we known.*
> *it isn't what happens in life,*
> *it's how you handle it."*
>
> -Unknown

My youngest son was deathly ill fighting for his life against an illness for which doctors had yet to find a cure.

I spent twenty of each twenty-four hours in his room in Isolation. I reassured him, cared for him and entertained him with my musical instruments, puppets and Storytelling when he was awake. When he was asleep, I napped, practiced my Tai Chi Chih movements, meditated and prayed. I also researched and prepared the format and stories I would tell on my own syndicated family TV show, RUTHMARIE'S ROOM.

My audience of adults and children were used to my happy, upbeat attitude, positive images and stories of humor. It was very difficult at this time to wipe the tears and continue this image every day in front of the taping cameras.

We changed my on-location programs to a closed-set studio with no live audience during this hectic time, so I had to imagine my audience watching and reacting.

As troublesome as these weeks were before a cure was discovered to help my son's illness, I know this was another period of my life during which my stories helped me. I purposefully chose stories that spoke to me, as well as to my listeners, of hope, faith, love and happiness. My stories helped me survive my tragedy.

The Storyteller: For and About All Ages

The following is excerpted from a lecture I gave at a university:

"The Arts, I believe, if used as loving tools, can help to solve most every human problem. We should be increasing their involvement more in our daily life, not cutting back support. And, I'm talking about heavy-duty communication ideas of world understanding, prosperity, peace and love, as well as indirect ways to assist starvation, housing, improved health and living standards.

The Art of Storytelling, being one of the most universally used and personally shared, has one of the heaviest responsibilities for the future world.

Diplomacy of the New Age will have, I perceive, the offerings of well trained, deeply motivated Storytellers with huge, instantly recalled repertoires or abilities to extemporize new stories to help negotiations and options open to mankind.

Freedom of choice must be based on information, intuition and new choices. Even today, the Art of Storytelling is the most growing art of practitioners involved in education, entertainment, literature, folklore and religious fields. More and more people of all ages are enjoying and getting involved in festivals, radio, tapes, TV, schools and in all kinds of public speaking opportunities.

Like all new areas, there needs to be more involvement of sincere artists and recognition of versatile Storytellers who are masters of their art.

However, it is an art that, frequently, the older you are, the better you may be, based on life's experiences having tremendous value in imagery. Practice of techniques, organization of material, and attention to continuity of the story needs special attention, as well as who the story is directed to.

Storytelling has suffered by being lumped together with Theater-Drama and Library Arts in most universities and funding sources.

It is an important contributor to those schools, but Storytelling needs to be more and more honored as its own separate Art form. More ancient in form than most others, it is practiced more in today's modern daily life than most others, except, perhaps music.

Like others, it has its amateurs, part-timers, and all other levels of expertise. The proof is in the telling and the results expected.

Meeting planners, conference and seminar coordinators, dinner and party bookers, all should consider the involvement of more Storyteller artists to add a new dimension of joy and understanding.

Some of us are 'custom-producers' of Storytelling programs. If I am given enough time, I will find or originate stories suitable to any needs for any age or cause I agree to.

People have asked how I keep such high energy while raising a wonderful, large family and traveling all over the world for many years as a Storyteller.

I believe in my stories! I renew my faith in God daily. I laugh a lot. I practice daily my 20 movements of Tai Chi Chih, as developed by Justin Stone, and of which I am also a certified teacher. These easily learned exercises I can do just about any place and renew my circulation balance of 'Chi' energy, good health, all of which are available to any of us who will make the effort.

My success in being a Storyteller Artist all over the world has broadened into even 'other worlds' of interest, as I age. I am becoming more and more interested in areas of 'New Age' thinking and possibilities of supreme enlightenment of spiritual insights by using my Art form for Re-Creation to help others."

Amongst other offers after this talk, I was immediately asked to use my art form to assist professional swim teams to overcome difficulties, which was successfully done. I was asked to participate in CONTACT, a worldwide annual conference of anthropologists, astro-physicists, NASA experts and top science-fiction writers, which I excitedly did.

I was asked to perform at an "International Romance Conference" in Hawaii on a Love Boat. Since I am already a "romantic lover," it was a real challenge to interweave "Universal Love" in this fun booking.

How?

Well, these are all only a few of my many Re-Creation stories to share another time.

Like the tiny birds, we are always in His Hands.

The stories yet unlived, yet untold, are the
Great Adventure.

Harold R. McAlindon
The Innovation Institute
Midtown Plaza,Suite 316
1717 West End Ave.
Nashville, TN 37203
(615) 329-4849

Harold McAlindon

Harold McAlindon (Mack-a-lin-don) is currently president of The Innovation Institute and Development Associates of Nashville, Tennessee. He has been selected as one of the top management speakers in America by the International Platform Association, the President's Association, and the World Future Society. His concepts and strategies have won many national awards including the Torch Award of A.S.T.D. and the Creative Application Award of ASPA.

Harold has been featured on programs with such leading authorities as Peter Drucker, Edward DeBono, Paul Harvey, and Norman Vincent Peale. He has served as senior consultant with such organizations as IBM, the Federal Reserve Board, National Office of the YMCA, American Institute of Banking, Blue Cross, General Foods, plus numerous hospitals, universities, business and religious organizations.

The Thomas Jefferson Research Center selected Harold to speak at their Frontiers of Management Program. The World Future Society selected him as a featured speaker for the World Conference in Washington DC.

Harold has had more than 75 articles featured in the Advanced Management Journal, Creative Living, Success Unlimited, *and other respected journals. His book,* Getting the Most Out of Your Job and Your Organization *was published by AMACOM. Success Motivation Institute is distributing a cassette version of this book and other works by Harold.*

An avid jogger and reader, Harold is married and has two children.

Enhancing
Innovative Performance

By Harold R. McAlindon

*"The time has now come to do for innovation
what we first did for management in general:
To develop the principles, the practice, and the discipline."*
- Peter F. Drucker

We are not really entering an era of innovation. Innovation has always been our fuel of progress. Everything that we have and everything that we have accomplished began as ideas. Visionary and courageous people converted these ideas into tangible and positive change. The history of America, or any progressive country, quickly demonstrates the power and potential of innovation. What we have not had, however, is a systematic way of harnessing and directing this magnificent force for good. Indeed this is the personal and professional challenge that we all face. The ability to create and innovate in an active, rather than a reactive, manner opens unlimited possibilites for the future. We now have the communications capability, the technology, and the distribution systems to put creativity and innovation techniques within everyone's reach. The key to unlocking this potential, however, is still an internal one. Unless we see the importance, the value and the potential from a personal point of view, few of us will be moved to take the initiative to lead this movement. This situation was a major motivating force for the founding of the Innovation Institute in Nashville, Tennessee.

The Innovation Institute

At our Nashville-based Innovation Institute, we have created a series of programs and services to promote strategic thinking, creativity, innovation, and entrepreneurship as teachable skills. The basic teaching process is a familiar one. It involves the utilization of various techniques in simulated situations until participants are comfortable with them. Once the participants have demonstrated their basic competence with the concepts, the skills are applied to real life situations and issues. The goals are: To solve problems, create opportunity, and enrich the human condition through applied thought. Our belief is that applied thought is potentially our most productive form of labor.

Our Slogan: *"Innovation creates opportunity, quality creates demand, and teamwork makes it happen."* The institute is also a vehicle that provides us with the opportunity to network with other individuals and organizations that are interested in promoting thinking, creativity, and innovation as professional disciplines. The Innovation Institute administers the C.P.I. (Certified Professional Innovator) examination to ghose seeking professional recognition of their ability.

Strategic Thinking

The most important activity in the world today is the teaching of thinking. The condition of the world is a reflection of our individual and collective thought. The effort and investment we make to improve our quality of thought is a barometer of what the quality of our future will be. If we look at thinking as a professional skill, the quality of our thinking can be improved like any other skill. There are many kinds of thinking techniques; creative thinking, positive thinking, logical thinking, negative thinking, lateral thinking, and group thinking, to name a few. Each method has its advantages, but each also has its limitations. To limit ourselves to any one method is to severely handicap our management of opportunity. The various kinds of thinking can all be put into three broad categories: Insight, Sequential, and Strategic.

"Insight" is the "aha" experience. When we experience "Insight," the method of arriving at a solution is not apparent.

The second category of thinking, "Sequential Thinking," is the process where specific steps lead to a predictable answer.

Finally, "Strategic Thinking" is decision making from a wide variety of created options. It is this process of maximizing and utilizing options that offers us unlimited promise. Individuals with an understanding of each of the various thought strategies and techniques can collectively utilize the ones that are appropriate for specific issues or situations. This also works wonders with group dynamics.

Steps to Improve Thinking Skills

In order to improve our thinking we can all take some fundamental steps:

    1. You must want to improve your thinking. Unless YOU are motivated to improve and see the importance of your mental skills, everything else is academic. Make a commitment to improve your thinking.

2. **Thinking must be viewed as a skill.**
   The potential that we have as individuals varies, but there is little doubt that we can all improve. If we look at thinking as a specific skill, we can isolate it, evaluate it, and improve it the same way we can a" backhand" or a "putt."

3. **We must learn some basic techniques.**
   There are many different "kinds of thinking" and many tested techniques for exercising our mental muscles. The more of these we are familiar and comfortable with, the better off we will be. Positive thinking, creative thinking, logical thinking and lateral thinking are but a few. Each method has its strengths and limitations.

4. **We must practice our thinking skill.**
   We improve our thinking skills by using them, not by being lectured at. Our thinking "practice" should include a wide variety of situations so that we can apply the necessary skill to the appropriate issue or situation.

5. **We must set aside time to think.**
   Unless we set aside time to think, our mental energies will be spent in re-active rather than active directions. They also tend to be utilized in "solving problems" rather than "creating opportunity." Set aside at least 30 minutes per day as think time. During this time jot down your ideas and perceptions. This becomes your idea bank.

Creativity

Do you agree with Albert Einstein that "imagination is more important than knowledge." I don't! That statement has been frequently debated. Few of us would disagree, however, that knowledge imaginatively utilized has more potential than knowledge that is viewed in a static way. In this booming information age, this fact is vitally important. Enhancing personal, group, and organizational creativity is the foundation from which successful innovation efforts spring. Creativity is not the end in itself. Creativity is the beginning of the process.

Creativity must be focused. The value of thinking up ideas and novel ways of doing things is good mental exercise. In a business setting, however, our goal is to produce results. A prominent advertising agency once used the slogan, "If it doesn't sell...it ain't creative." In business, creativity must contribute to our mission, philosophy, and goals.

"Ideation" and "innovation" are not synonymous. "Ideation" deals with the generation of ideas while "innovation" reflects the implementation of ideas as change, new products, or new processes. It is the constant lack of awareness of this distinction that is responsible for much of the static practices of our corporations. Ideas become the end result rather than the beginning of the process. Innovation does not have to have a pre-determined guarantee of success. In fact, to require in advance that there be no doubt of its success would disable its chance of ever being tried. Well defined evaluation criteria will go a long way toward helping to improve our success ratio.

Whatever the goals of business may be, it must make money. To do that we must get things done. Having ideas is seldom equivalent to getting things done in the business or organization sense. Ideas do not implement themselves... people implement ideas.

Steps to Improve Creativity

All people have untapped creative ability. Ideas are always the starting point of progress. The following strategies can help us improve our creative output.

1. **Provide Incentives.**

   Creativity flows in the direction of rewards. When creativity is encouraged, recognized, and rewarded, we tend to get more of it. Provide monetary rewards for creativity.

2. **Solicit Ideas.**

   Ask people for their thoughts on specific issues, problems, or opportunites. If people sense that you "expect" them to be creative they are more likely to contribute their suggestions and insights. Have idea "events," meetings, and management or employee discussion groups.

3. **Brainstorm.**

   This is one of the oldest, yet most successful methods of promoting creativity. People can spark each other and, together, can create whole ideas from fragments. A word of caution:

the sessions should follow specific guidelines and be professionally led to generate the best results.

4. **Utilize mental exercises.**
   Provide your staff with puzzles, games, and challenges to help promote a "Spirit of Creativity." The Innovation Institute has an excellent variety of these available.

Innovation

The ability to convert ideas into tangible change, products and services requires a specific set of skills and techniques. Innovation is a group process. Without a "system" of innovation, ideas are never fully developed. Ideas get discussed in the coffee shop, during breaks, etc. They will not, however, become that new business possibility. Unless the members of the group have a uniform understanding of the criteria and techniques that are to be employed, the result will be confusion.

Innovation also requires that members of the team be able to interact effectively. This is a result of group leadership as well as the selection process for team members.

Most executives want their companies to be more competitive, not in just one or two dimensions, but across the board. What can we do to raise our innovative batting averages in the area of establishing and maintaining our creative advantage?

Innovation must not limit itself to research and development departments. Research is only one tool of innovation.

Innovation requires:

1. The sloughing off of yesterday
2. The systematic search for innovative opportunities
3. The willingness to set up the innovative venture.

The organization that organizes for innovation will have an advantage on the competition. The future will be dominated by change. Change presents the innovator with the arena to apply innovative skills.

Steps to a Productive Innovative Team

1. Members must be compatible
2. They should be people who are capable of "making things happen"
3. They should be friendly, open, positive, and loose
4. They should be "active" participants
5. They should have the necessary skills for the project
6. The originator of the idea being processed should be in attendance
7. The group must accept the fact that no one has a patent on good ideas or information
8. The team must know their specific reason for working together

9. The members must be accountable as a unit within a larger framework
10. The members must know that they need each others' skills.

Entrepreneurship

The ability to turn ideas into bank deposits is what entrepreneurship is all about. Enlightened organizations are creating "Intrapreneurship" strategies. This gives employees and staff members the opportunity to create new businesses without having to leave the organization to do it. There are many variations of this strategy but they all include three important success strategies:
1. A top management commitment to change.
2. An allocation of organizational resources to well developed "high potential" ideas.
3. Putting the person with the idea "in charge" of the idea.

The Innovative Organization

Individuals cannot innovate. People can come up with all kinds of ideas and fragments of ideas. Ideas, however, are not innovations. Innovation is change, or products, or services that result from a diverse group blending their talents to "develop" ideas and to consider all aspects of them. Ideas must be looked at and evaluated utilizing a broad range of criteria before they can be considered a viable candidate for innovation. Once the innovation has been developed, it then requires the resources of the organization to bring it to the marketplace, to manage it, and to abandon it when its life cycle has been completed. The organizations that enjoy successful innovation efforts recognize these three realities and operate within their parameters.

Innovation is a matter of survival. Being innovative some of the time in one or two areas will not get the job done. We must consider innovation the primary resource for keeping our organization and its people focused, challenged, and productive in all aspects of the operation. Innovation must be seen as an organizational norm. Creating a culture of innovation is the best competitive tool a company can have.

The Essentials of Innovation

1. Top management must be commited to innovation. If they are not, they shouldn't be in top management. Without innovation, the organization is doomed to fail.
2. Organizational resources must be made available to exploit innovative opportunites.
3. Organizations must abandon the "old" and the "dying" to make resources available for tomorrow's champions.

4. Creativity and innovation flow in the direction of rewards. There must be an incentive to be creative.
5. There must be a system in place to evaluate, develop, process, and support ideas.
6. Innovation must be organized outside the spectrum of day-to-day operations.
7. People must understand the dynamics of innovation and be able to live with them.
8. There must be a person responsible for innovation — a Chief Innovation Officer (C.I.O.).
9. People must be trained in creative and innovative techniques and strategies.
10. Innovation must be measured. They must be, however, measured in total. One huge success can offset a high number of "failures."
11. Before attempting to innovate, make sure the desired result does not already exist somewhere else.
12. It is important to judge innovation in terms of quality and impact rather than quantity.

Three Different Examples of Success

The following examples help to illustrate three different approaches to creativity and innnovation by three very different styles of executive in three very diverse businesses. All three are very succesful in their own way:

The Visionary Leader

Sam L. Moore is one of the south's most innovative leaders. A former top salesman with IBM, Mr. Moore now directs Corporate Environments, Inc. and Moore Acquisition Company. He is also a partner in the Innovation Institute. Sam recognized the dynamics of the business environment and has committed his company to integrating innovation into its daily operating culture. Mr. Moore established innovation "quotas" for his staff and provided financial incentives to motivate them. His staff is trained in strategic thinking, creativity, and innovation techniques. Mr. Moore recognizes that quality and performance standards can never be static. Innovation becomes the life blood of the organization that keeps organizational performance and priorities at the cutting edge of the market place. The result is a dynamic, vibrant, service-oriented company that has created an internal insurance policy against failure.

Changing the Perspective

Sometimes a different focus can help maximize performance. Mr. George Wade, dynamic general manager of Shared Hospital Services in Nashville, Tennessee (which processes more laundry in one hour than a family of four does in two years) is a good case in point. Mr. Wade says, "Our product is laundry, but our business is service." His entire staff is viewed as a group of service representatives. He also views his supervisors as "teachers" and trains them to be teachers. The result is that his supervisors are better prepared to develop the performance potential of their staffs.

It is no surprise that with this type of leadership, Shared Hospital Services enjoys a national reputation for excellence and serves as a virtual role model for effective laundry and service management.

Divine Guidance

Mr. Jack Kerls, a St. Louis businessman, is a rare kind of individual in many ways. He believes in prayer, seeking God's guidance for the running of his company. Mr. Kerls says the Bible has all the answers we need for our lives, including our daily business practices. I have had the privilege of consulting for this fine group of people. It is a humbling and inspiring experience to hear the president of the company, Mr. Kerls, open a meeting with a prayer requesting guidance, wisdom, inspiration, and successful outcome for the session. This practice formulates an excellent foundation for the creativity of the group. The results of these meetings have been new products, innovative marketing strategies, and new manufacturing technologies and systems. Mr. Kerls' idea is, "why go it alone when you can depend on a truly loving God, who cares for us and wants to be a part of our lives if we will only let Him."

The Follow-through

Creativity without action-oriented follow-through is a very barren form of individual behavior. In a sense it is even irresponsible. This is so because...

1. The creative person who tosses out ideas and does little in terms of implementation, is shirking responsibility for one of the prime requsites of business... action.
2. By avoiding follow-through we behave in an organizationally intolerable fashion ... sloppily.

The trouble with much creativity today is that many of the people with ideas have the peculiar notion that their jobs are finished when they suggest them; that it is up to somebody else to work out the dirty details and implement the proposals.

"Creativity" is not the "miraculous" road to business growth and affluence that many claim it to be. For the line manager particularly, it can be a millstone rather than a milestone. The trouble with much of the advice business gets today about the need to be more vigorously creative is that its advocates often fail to distinguish between creativity and innovation. Creativity THINKS UP new things. Innovation DOES new things. The difference speaks for itself. Yet most of us still rate ideas more by their novelty than by their practicability. Too often we mistake the idea for a great painting with the great painting itself.

Anybody who knows anything about organizations knows how hard it is to get things done, let alone introduce new ways of doing things, no matter how promising they seem. A powerful new idea can kick around unused for years, not because its merits are not recognized, but because nobody has assumed the responsibility for converting it from words into action. What is lacking is not creativity in the idea-creating sense but innovation in the action- producing sense. The ideas are not being put to work. There is no center of entrepreneurial energy.

Measuring Our Performance

Creativity, innovation, and entrepreneurship must be measured as other management functions and contributions are. We must:

1. Get market and operational feedback that measures actual results against expectations.
2. Have a systematic review of innovative efforts all together. Innovation is not just a group of products and services, but organizational and systems changes as well.
3. Evaluate our entrepreneurial performance against our objectives, budgets, standing in the market and the entire business.

One significant innovative success can offset many failures. We must never lose sight of that fact.

The Future of innovation

The organization of the future will have a Chief Innovation Officer (C.I.O.) who will enjoy the same executive status as the Chief Financial Officer or Chief Marketing Officer. The business of the future will recognize that the abbreviation "R.O.I" not only represents "Return on Investment" but also, "Return on Innovation." Innovation, creativity, and effective thinking skills will become educational necessities and will be part of the curriculum of responsible schools at all levels. Executive training programs will have standard components that deal with creativity, innovation, and strategic thinking. There will be a "gold collar" status of worker to replace blue collar and white collar workers. As mentioned earlier, the Innovation Institute administers the C.P.I. (Certified Professional Innovator) examination to help professionalize the function.

Ultimately, innovation will become an integral part of the fabric of our daily lives. As we master our mental potential, integrate it with others and utilize technology to support it — we are in fact mastering our future. Henry David Thoreau once said that, "to impact the quality of the day" was our greatest ability. The Creative Innovators will be leaders of that movement.

Mindpower is to the information age what iron, coke, and oil were to the industrial age — the one necessary ingredient on thich all else depends. While brainpower was taken for granted by leaders of the industrial revolution, brainpower is now sought and competed for by corporations as an essential to their success. To gain and maintain a competitive edge in today's environment, managers must learn to tap this vital resource.

The Value of It All

If people are taught to think strategically, enhance creativity, and convert innovations into progress and prosperity — the economic impact would be tremendous. We must not lose sight, however, of the fact that the health and happiness of people everywhere would also be elevated.

The innovative organization, the organization that resists stagnation rather than change, is a major challenge to management, private and public. That such organizations are possible, we can assert with confidence, because there are enough of them around.

The right way to address this issue so as to make it capable of resolution is as a challenge to create, build, and maintain the innovative organization, the organization for which change is norm rather than exception, and opportunity rather than threat.

As we look to the organization of the future, we are looking at perhaps the most important vehicle for social and economic progress that we have. If we commit ourselves to organizations that release rather than surpress human potential, initiative, and creativity — it will be exciting to be a part of the organization of the future.

Carolyn B. Finch
Bogart Communications
51 Cedar Drive
Danbury, CT 06811
(203) 744-6518   (203) 792-4833

Carolyn B. Finch

Carolyn B. Finch is a Connecticut licensed Speech/Language Pathologist, a successful speaker, educator, businesswoman and entrepreneur. She started her first business at age 12 when she began washing and waxing cars. She sold cosmetics in college and since then she has founded Peter Piper School and Learning Center Inc. (a preschool, kindergarten and speech clinic). This was the first school to mainstream handicapped children in Connecticut. Speech Pathology Associates was an outgrowth of this program. Carolyn established eighteen other speech programs in Western Connecticut. Educational 'N Therapeutic Materials, a mail order business was established and The Sunshine Shop, a retail store. Both businesses specialized in materials for the learning disabled and speech handicapped.

Carolyn has her B.S. in Early Childhood Education and Speech Therapy from Elmira College and her M.S. in Elementary Education and Communication from Western Connecticut State University. Her present business, Bogart Communications, conducts seminars, workshops, offers services for speech improvement, public speaking, foreign dialect improvement and speech and language therapy. Carolyn is author of Portraits of Sounds, Speech Therapy at Home, *a correspondence course,* The I Love You Dictionary of Four Letter Words *and* Universal Handtalk®, *a system of 48 signs to use for emergency.*

She is also director of the Institute of Communication Conseling® (a Correspondence Speech Correction Program), and is an adjunct Professor at Western Connecticut State Univesity. Carolyn is an active member of the Fairfield County 4-H Advisory Board in Connecticut and is an Incorporator and Director for Liberty National Bank. She has been named to 1988-89 Who's Who of American Women *and is the wife of Market Researcher Donald Hulme. They are the parents of four college-age students.*

Universal Handtalk®

By Carolyn Finch

*"Making the simple complicated is commonplace;
Making the complicated simple, awesomely simple, that's
creativity."*

- Charles Mingus

It was a beautiful evening when the fire broke out. I
didn't think it was anything exceptional as I drove
past the billowing clouds of smoke. However, the next
day I learned that two firemen had died because of
miscommunication. When the fire broke out the
custodian in the factory ran to a bar next door to
report the fire. No one understood what he was trying

to say because he had been in this country from southeast Asia only one month. The bartender told me later that, "he waved his arms and talked in a language I couldn't understand." The custodian ran off to find a friend who knew his language. Meanwhile the fire department arrived and so did the factory manager. The manager told the fire chief there was a "man in there." Two firefighters went in. The ceiling caved in and they were both killed.

I was angry. Those firemen had died in vain. I took my research off the shelf and continued to work to develop the Survival Sign System (as it was called then) that I had begun seven years before.

The Beginning

I set up the cards, tested them around the country and used them in hospitals and clinics where I worked.

I was called in to help a patient who had a bullet in his head. Psychologically, he was afraid to move his head for fear the bullet would "blow up." I taught him to communicate with hand gestures down along the side of the bed. Hallelujah! He was able to communicate. This made the nurses' work easier and the present owner of the bullet learned to feel a little more relaxed because he could communicate.

I soon found that this system could be used during the "circle time" in nursery schools and thus save continued interruptions to go to the potty! I used it at distances to communicate and most of all I could train the mentally handicapped to use these gestures and have fun doing them.

Teachers from Literacy Voluteers have used the system and I am presently using the system with speech therapy, foreign speaking, to gesture over noise pollution and training firefighters.

Universal Handtalk® is not a language. It is a *system* to enhance communication. When the hospital called and said there was a referral from a physician to use my system, I was delighted. In about twenty minutes this wonderful man was able to verbalize "I love you" to his wife and his daughter by using finger pointing and outstretched thumb and pinky.

The next day I received a phone call from the hospital that the patient had died. What a wonderful gift he had given to his family!

Perhaps Universal Handtalk® can help you, a loved one or a friend to enhance, replace or develop more communication.

you, you plural, your, you're

Which Came First, Body Language or Speech?

We don't know which came first, the spoken word or gestures. However, it is likely that gestures are the oldest forms of communication. There has been considerable study recently as to how individuals develop speech and speech patterns.

It is my opinion, based on study, research and development of gestures, that body language was the first form of communication.

Egyptian drawings depict body gestures used by people in ancient civilizations. A study of the famous and not so famous works of art depict many basic gestures. As a society we all have gestures and hand signs that we use regularly. Early explorers communicated with natives using gestures. Many of these gestures were recorded in ship's logs.

Indians of the Americas used gestures and signs to communicate within a tribe while hunting. If they spoke during that time it could frighten game. This was their way of surviving. Indian languages differed but Indians from other tribes could communicate using their knowledge of body language. This is the same way travelers express their needs when in a country where they do not speak the language.

What Are Signs and Gestures?

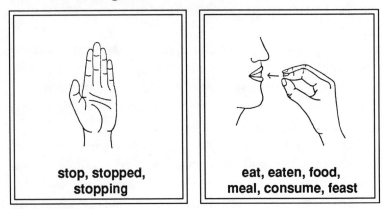

| stop, stopped, stopping | eat, eaten, food, meal, consume, feast |

Signs:

They are nonverbal posters or boards that send a message to the viewer. They are hand movements that are signals and transmit a message. They are messages from the eyes sent to the viewer.

Gestures:

They are motions with the limbs or body that transmit a certain message. They are hand motions that are used socially to signal messages.

Sign Language:

This is an established language like any language which has been organized for use by a specific group of individuals. The group includes deaf students, family, friends and teachers. (However, not all deaf people use sign language and they don't all use the same method.)

Sign Systems:

A group of signs and/or gestures that are used by a specific group of individuals to enhance communication due to environmental disturbances. There are about 33 sign systems that are used daily by various groups. These are used to enhance communication and deliver the appropriate message.

There are different sign systems for different sports. Baseball, football, soccer, basketball are some of the games that use sign systems. The voice is not capable of sending messages over a long distance with associate noise. There are sign systems used in aeronautics, underwater diving, with sandhogs, in the military and at the Stock Exchange.

Universal Handtalk ® :

This is a system combining the most appropriate hand signs from a variety of languages and other systems. This system can enhance any language individuals already know.

The system is used for emergency, those with limited speech, (speech impaired or foreign speaking) neurologically handicapped, and by those who cannot use their voice due to environmental discomfort and disturbances.

Nonverbal Communication Never Stops

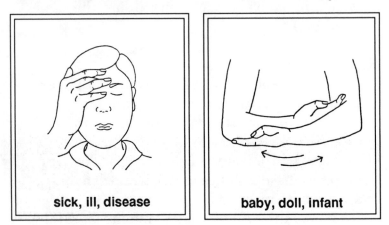

sick, ill, disease   baby, doll, infant

Today we all use gestures and signs to communicate feelings and needs. Researchers have discovered that at least 65% of messages that we interpret are nonverbal. Nonverbal communication sends messages. However, not all body language is interpreted appropriately.

When members of the speaking world are ill, restrained, medicated or handicapped they still must communicate. Sometimes gestures must be used to communicate needs rather than speech.

Universal Handtalk® is a grouping of appropriate signs for daily use. These signs and this gesture system can become a part of communication for those who need to express emergency wants and needs.

Sick, Injured and EMTs

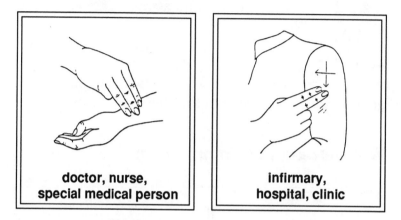

| doctor, nurse, special medical person | infirmary, hospital, clinic |

A sick or injured individual has been comfortable in his world and suddenly is hospitalized. He has been a private person and now people are invading his body, his private world. He is probed, injected, bathed and assisted to the bathroom. In extreme cases, individuals need assistance in eating (getting food into their mouths and swallowing). Usually this is due to muscle control. Others need help in the ability to communicate their needs and wants. Some individuals are born with severe problems and are deprived of the ability to speak. They have a need to communicate their needs and wants.

Some individuals speak no English, the major language of the United States. Universal Handtalk® is composed of signs that are interrelated. They were chosen to be used as a temporary or permanent system of communication. The ideas, principles and procedures of this system are explained on the following pages. It may be used as a universal system of communication.

There have been several devised, revised and expanded sign language systems and programs that incorporate a variety of signs for the deaf population, government sign systems and teaching systems.

We All Need to Communicate

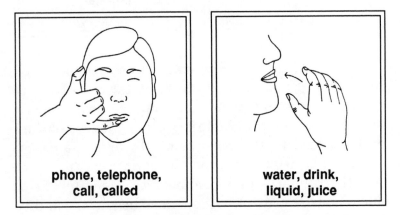

| phone, telephone, call, called | water, drink, liquid, juice |

People with varied backgrounds have the same basic needs in life. A primary need is to communicate. The mouth expresses words and language. The body expresses gestures and language.

A combination of sign, gesture, and speech, is total communication. Universal Handtalk®, is a combination of sign, gesture and speech, it is a total communication system incorporating forty-eight signs. Hearing individuals can use the system to communicate their needs in case of sickness, disease and other emergencies concerning themselves or others.

Universal Handtalk® is the result of 9 years of research and 5 years sales under the name "The Survival Sign System."

History of Signs and Gestures

time, hour, clock, late

Fingerspelling is a system of communication that has been used since earliest Christian times. This system uses various hand and finger positions to represent the letters of the alphabet. Due to their vows of silence, monks of the Middle Ages communicated with each other using this method. Tenth century Latin Bibles show drawings of the various hand positions. This method was adapted for English and called the Manual Alphabet. It was further adapted for the deaf in the Rochester System.

Indians Signed

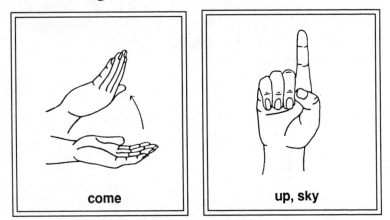

Indian Handtalk is a system developed by the American Plains Indians. Iron Eyes Cody, a Cherokee Indian, learned the system and recorded the signs in his writings. This is the system learned by boys in scouting organizations today.

Sign Language For the Deaf

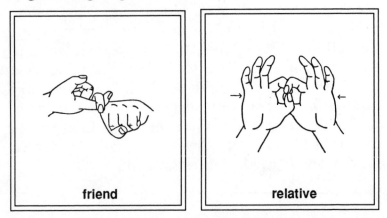

Language of Signs was considered to be invented by Abbe Charles de l'Eppe. He published his Language of Signs and method of teaching the deaf. He is considered Father of the language of signs and was instrumental in establishing the first school for the deaf in Paris in 1760. This system continued in Europe during the 18th and 19th centuries.

American Language of Signs is an adaptation of the French system that Dr. Thomas Hopkins Gallaudet had observed while visiting Abbe de l'Eppe's school in France. The American Language of Signs was being used in 1817 when the American School for the Deaf was established in Hartford, Connecticut. The system expanded into higher education when Edward Miner Gallaudet established Gallaudet College, the world's first and only college for the deaf in Washington, D.C. The charter for the college was signed by President Abraham Lincoln in 1864. Perhaps that is why the statue in the Lincoln Memorial shows the President's hands spelling A.L.

American Sign Language is the established language of communication for the adult deaf in North America. This has been used for over 100 years. Parts of it have been used by hearing persons in noisy locations, under water and in sports. This language is based on natural gestures of the deaf. However, signs are continually being changed or invented. American Sign Language must be learned like any other language. It presently is accepted as a language requirement in many graduate schools in the United States. This system includes pantomime and a considerable amount of body language.

Various Sign Systems

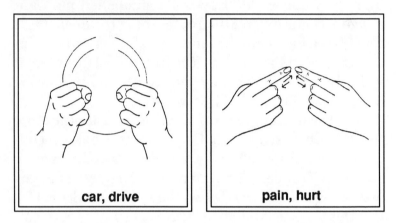

car, drive   pain, hurt

Systematic Sign Language was developed by Richard Paget. He was the first to develop a manual representation of English words. He worked in England in the 1930's and 40's and published the Systematic Sign Language in 1951. He maintained that a sign system should follow the order of our speech, as portrayed in the English language. Some of the signs he developed he felt could be used internationally.

The Paget-Gorman Sign System is an advanced form of the Systematic Sign Language. This system was renamed after Pierre Gorman, an Australian, who continued to use and enlarge the system.

Seeing Essential English was a program developed by David Anthony after he used American Sign Language and The Manual Alphabet when he worked with deaf, retarded individuals. These experiences were the basis for Seeing Essential English which represents sound, spelling and meaning of parts of English words. There is a similar system called Signing Exact English.

Signed English is a system intended to be an "aid" to language acquisition for the deaf. It is directed to the preschool and elementary levels of education. Signed English uses the gestures of signs and markers. Each sign represents a word spoken. The markers indicate plurals, tense and possessives. Signed English is a combination of American Sign Language symbols, Seeing Essential English and signs developed from the Gallaudet community.

Visual signal systems are varied. They include the use of lights such as traffic signals, flags as in boating and auto racing, and hand and body movements. Most major sports have standard signal systems used by officials to communicate various plays and moves of the games. Board of Trade hand signals are used in the stock market to buy and sell.

American Indian Gestural Code (Amerind) is a system based upon the American Indian Sign Language. This system was used and developed by Madge Skelly, a speech pathologist. She used this program with stroke patients and others who were speech-handicapped.

Universal Handtalk®

help

Universal Handtalk® is an emergency communication system combining Indian systems, daily emblem signs and the help sign created by the author.

This system is based upon 26 years of experience using "sign" with the speech handicapped in hospitals, clinics and home settings. Universal Handtalk® was formerly The Survival Sign System©. It has been used with speech handicapped clients for 10 years. It is mentioned in a new book by Rodale Press, *The I Love You Dictionary of Four Letter Words* and other publications.

A small Universal Handtalk® pocket guide and wall posters are available for sale from Bogart Communications, 36 Tamarack Ave., Suite 335, Danbury, CT 06811. Telephone: (203) 790-6457

Universal Handtalk®, a "Survival Sign System" incorporates signs that can be easily learned and used by any person who is capable of learning. Signs from the program have already been taught to aphasic, autistic, mentally retarded, hard of hearing, and those with poor volume and muscle control.

The signs can also be used for communication by firefighters, police and ambulance drivers. But most importantly, this system is for the hearing population to use when it is necessary to communicate needs and wants without speech. It is best to use one hand for signs whenever possible.

At this time, handicapped persons are being mainstreamed into society. They are in schools, work programs, they travel and are on public transportation. They must be understood! The elderly are rapidly increasing as a group and they are more independent and therefore travel and have greater needs to communicate.

We have more foreign speaking people in our environment than ever and they have a need for instant communication. Universal Handtalk® is the system that can be used worldwide in schools, fire departments, factories, medical facilities and travel associated businesses and all should have access to this program.

I love you

Thank you for the opportunity to share this system.

Don Uker
The Don Uker Company, Inc.
107 Morningside Drive
Denison, IA 51442
712 263-2357

Don Uker

Don Uker was born and raised in the Chicago suburbs. His father was a civil engineer and former vaudeville magician. His mother was a homemaker and the daughter of an Oklahoma land rush pioneer.

Uker was one of the first graduates of the Radio and Television curriculum at Iowa State University. During college he worked concurrently as announcer for three different radio stations, serving as classical music commentator, newsman, and originator of his own comedy show. He was employed at the local television station, where he rose to director during his final year. He also wrote for the college humor magazine.

He served two years in France as Signal Corps Photographer, and returned to Iowa where he worked and eventually became involved in the ownership of broadcast properties in Denison and Des Moines.

He has served as president of the Iowa Broadcasters Association and the Iowa Radio Network. He is the recipient of many state and local community service awards.

In 1980 he formed his own media company through which he does media and advertising consulting and prepares and presents multi-image audio-visual shows.

He presents a seminar on advertising and speaks at many banquets, meetings, and conventions.

Developing the Ability to Think Creatively

By Don Uker

*"If a man does not keep pace with his companions,
perhaps it is because he hears a different drummer.
Let him step to the music which he hears,
however measured or far away."*
- Henry D. Thoreau, *Walden*

I remember as a young boy growing up in the Chicago suburbs and taking long walks hand in hand with my mother. She would stop suddenly, turn, and look longingly upwards into the sky at the clouds... and then turn to me and ask me what I saw up there.

At first I saw nothing, just odd shaped clusters of vapor. When I reported this, she would quickly chastise me and then begin a long, detailed description of what she saw up there.

She would describe the face of a giant in military head dress, casting his stern gaze toward a herd of elephants as they approached the precipice guarded by regal lions. Soon I would be caught up in her description and adding my own observations... "Why was the giant mad? Will the lions prevent their advance?"

We've all had similar experiences. I was fortunate to have a mother who first of all allowed me to share in her creative experience and secondly encouraged me to look for and find my own pictures in the sky.

Now as an adult, charged with the responsibilities of earning a living, having been subjected to a structured education, and facing the relentless pressures of day to day existence... suddenly when I look up into the sky all I see are banks of cumulus clouds.

The bad news is... now I have to concentrate to see the giant. The good news is...the giant is still there if you look for him.

The great news is... all of the excitement is in trying to find him.

Breaking Out of the Molds

Each of us is caught up in our daily life, victimized by the experiences and education we've had. As we grew and matured, we faced problem after problem and we developed ways of solving or coping with them. Some of our solutions worked well, others not quite so well. Life's experiences taught us to save the good solutions, storing them within our memory to be used again in "like" situations.

We developed a "memory bank" and "patterns" of "situational response" which serve us well for the most part, but limit us greatly when we endeavor to respond in a creative fashion. The sum of our experience and education has locked us into doing things the way we've always done them before.

*"Creative thinking may mean simply
the realization that there's no particular
virtue in doing things the way they always
have been done."*
- Rudolf Flesch

Each of us developed patterns for dealing with the events we encountered as we grew, as we learned, and as we passed through our individual world of work. Training ourselves to think creatively means breaking those chains which bind and limit us to only those solutions or ideas which have worked in the past.

We have to learn to open up and expand our "mind-set" before we can prepare ourselves for thinking creatively.

One of the devices which can be very helpful is our old stand-by..."P.M.A.," or Positive Mental Attitude.

Achieving and maintaining a positive mental attitude is perhaps the first step in discovering that anything is possible, in realizing that there may be a giant in the clouds after all. It helps us "clean the slate," and prepare our minds for thinking creatively. It establishes a "mind-set" in which the seeds for creative thinking can be planted and an atmosphere in which they might germinate and grow.

These seeds need to be nurtured. We can turn to another old friend for help with this. We can use the process of "visualization."

That means using our imagination to visualize our idea in reality, or in action. This process enables us to mentally construct the idea in our mind and to "see" how it works, to project the idea through our imagination, to examine it there, and to explore other possibilities.

Athletes use this system in developing their skills and talents... in essence they see themselves as winners and they become winners. Instead of just hoping they can have success and not embarrass themselves, they picture themselves as winners and achievers. They not only set their expectations high, but also envision themselves meeting and exceeding them.

You must not limit yourself with preconceptions of failure based on past experiences growing out of old molds. Preconceptions limit our ability to use visualization effectively. Visualizing yourself as a creative person is the first step in becoming a creative person.

Getting to "Anything Goes"

"Think before you speak is criticism's motto;
speak before you think creation's."
                                        - E. M. Foster

The truly creative person believes, that at least, in the embryo stage of an idea, "anything goes." It's using the "think-tank" concept at the grass roots level. Examining all of the "possible" and the "impossible" solutions, and considering everything before throwing anything out.

Learn to look at the situation from a unique or different angle. Consider how someone completely removed from the problem might react.

Creative people are persistent...they resist failure, but they understand that not everything works. They are more apt to ride the crest of an idea longer than others who may not be as patient or as believing.

Creative thinkers try not to let themselves be imprisoned by convention. They don't restrict their approaches to conventional routes... they try new highways.

They rebel at doing things the way they've always been done, if for no other reason except to be different. We are not opposed to constructing road blocks which are often self-imposed and cause us to seek new routes. We know that most of the creative excitement is in reaching the goal, and generally not in the goal itself.

Train yourself to look beyond the obvious questions. Try thinking a step ahead, anticipating direction. Try throwing the map away.

A true innovator on the trail of an imminent discovery will be a risk taker...risking becoming a cynic...risking exploiting ourselves and others in the hopes of precipitating an idea or a lead which will further the cause. A creative individual will risk a friendship and a relationship, perhaps his or her job, to elicit a response which will position their idea in a workable mode, or to generate within others an unconventional reaction, hopefully in a positive vein.

Living With the Fear of Loneliness

Creative people are often much like pioneers...off in remote areas discovering new continents. We are often faced with defending an idea that is ours alone and not shared or really understood or appreciated by others who have not yet broken from the bonds that hold them, or from the molds of convention.

Being a pioneer has never been completely safe, and those that choose safety shy from creativity.

"When I am...completely myself, entirely
alone...or during the night when I cannot sleep,
it is on such occasions that my ideas flow best
and most abundantly. Whence and
how these come I know not nor can I force them.
Nor do I hear in my imagination the parts
successively, but I hear them gleich alles zusammen.
(at the same time all together)."
- Wolfgang Amadeus Mozart

Discipline and Focused Awareness

In our efforts to develop our ability to think creatively we need to train ourselves to be receptive to new ideas and new concepts. We cannot maintain or fuel our creative energy if we close ourselves to external stimuli, new situations, or risk.

We need to train ourselves to be "multi-dimensional," that is to operate in at least two dimensions simultaneously...we need to be an actor in life and an observer of life at the same time. We need to be able to carry on our conversations and at the same time evaluate them and the situation with a focus on what we perceive as the goal.

"Discipline and focused awareness...
contribute to the act of creation."
- John Poppy

Using Time Wisely

I cannot always look into the sky and find giants, so I must understand that when I do see giants among the clouds I must record what I see. In other words, I must act when the creative mood strikes. Like Mozart, I cannot force creativity, but I can sometimes precipitate it or at least funnel my energy when the creative mood strikes.

When you have an idea or uncover a concept... record it. Always carry a tape recorder or a tablet on which to record your ideas and your reaction to stimuli. Don't ever rely on recording your feelings and ideas later, for they will never be the same.

Act now, for as time and attitude change, the idea will have lost its relativity, the environment will have changed, and what seemed like such a good idea will no longer appear as innovative. That may or may not be true, but you will not be in the proper, creative, "anything goes" frame of mind to evaluate it. I call it "diminished recollection," trying to recreate the mood, the feeling, the ambiance in which the creative idea unfolded. It doesn't work for me. I need to write it down when I get it, work on it when it happens, while the creative juices are flowing. Middle of the night, middle of a play, middle of a meal...whenever, wherever...write it down. The old tablet and pencil on the bed stand is still a good idea and it works.

Comfortable/Uncomfortable, Satisfied/Unsatisfied

> *"To be willing to suffer in order to create*
> *is one thing;*
> *to realize that one's creation necessitates*
> *one's suffering, that suffering is*
> *one of the greatest of God's gifts,*
> *is almost to reach a mystical solution of the*
> *problem of evil."*
> - J. W. N. Sullivan

There seems to be a universal feeling that all of us should always be, or at least strive for a situation in which we are always comfortable, satisfied and happy. It is my personal belief that such goals lead to creative mediocrity. When you are comfortable and satisfied, you are lulled into a state of restfulness. When you are uncomfortable and unsatisfied, you tend to seek to change your situation and the climate for creativity exists.

Someone once asked me if I was happy, and I replied that I was not happy and did not ever care to

be happy. All I want is the opportunity to search for happiness, for I know that in the search I will achieve the real feelings that most everyone associates with the goal. When and if I ever become happy, then I will quit searching for happiness, and then my creative life will have ended.

> *"Anxiety is the essential condition of intellectual and artistic creation.... and everything that is finest in human history."*
> - Charles Frankel

Develop the courage to lose battles while concentrating on the war. Learn how to pursue and persist in the light of apparent defeat. Learn how to celebrate the victory of small battles won...change is ever present, but sometimes slower than revolution.

> *"The most gifted members of the human species are at their best when they cannot have their way."*
> - Eric Hoffer

Train yourself to persist when those around you belittle your ideas because they either don't understand the problem, the method, or the creative process.

> *"Human salvation lies in the hands of the creatively maladjusted."*
> - Martin Luther King, Jr.

Breaking the Rules

In your search for creative ideas, break the rules. If not physically and outwardly... then in your mind and through visualization and imagination. Rules tend to promote structure and structure tends to prohibit creative thinking. As you release your mind from the structure of rules, and initiate your process of creative thinking, be sure to follow it through to its conclusion. Don't give up before you reach the end or after you find the first answer that works... look for the second or other "right" answers. Follow the axiom, "There's more than one way to skin a cat." There usually is.

Watch out for the villain who comes along and says, "We can't do it that way, we've never done it like that before."

Understand the limits of structure, both mentally and as it affects your capacity for leadership and entrepreneurial spirit. Remember, if you know how to add, when you add two plus two, you will always get four. But if you don't know how to add you can sometimes get five.

Consider where we might be today if the first settler who crossed the plains and spotted the Indians as they began their attack, had said, "Let's put the wagons in an isosceles triangle."

Creating the Creative Environment

I have learned that even though I may not feel in a creative mood, I can sometimes promote a feeling of creativity by placing myself in a creative atmosphere or environment. I have learned, by paying attention to past successes, that if I can place myself in a creative mode, my chances for success are greater. For me, that can mean moving physically to a place of great natural beauty, listening to music, either the familiar that I love or the unfamiliar that takes me to new places, or channeling my desires through the process of visualization, about success, love, about leadership, etc.

A fun working environment always produces more creativity than a dull one.

"One must not lose desires.
They are mighty stimulants to creativeness,
to love, and to long life."
- Alexander A. Bogomoletz

I have often used other devices to speed up the creative process. Let me share them with you. I can remember while writing advertising copy, being stumped, and having worked on a certain piece of copy for two weeks with virtually no results. As a last resort, I would call the client and tell him to be at my studio in one hour to review his new copy. That created a tremendous deadline and near panic pressure. But it also works for me... for invariably I will have something for him when he arrives. That system involves risk, such as losing the client should I fail to perform. But it also provides great reason to perform on schedule. It stimulates creativity, if you will.

I can remember other times sitting at the typewriter for hours waiting for that first sentence to materialize. I have since learned that it is far better to sit down and just start typing... anything, just get that first sentence down. Then the rest begins to flow, and I can always go back and change the first sentence.

Look for "cross-disciplinary" concepts, and turn them into ideas that will lead to your goals. This simply means looking for the answers to your problems in other places, not related to what you're searching for. If you are looking for a system in which to deliver inner office memos effectively, watch the paper boy organize his route.

Watch a roofer work his way to the top and learn how to apply his skills to constructing your boat dock, etc.

"It is the function of creative men
to perceive the relations
between thoughts, or things, or forms of expression
that may seem utterly different, and to be able

to combine them into some new forms...
the power to connect the seemingly unconnected."
  - William Plomer

Being creative means going further than everyone thinks you should, much like docking a boat in the wind. Sometimes you must drive the boat beyond the dock so that the winds of change will settle it into its mooring.

"There is a correlation between the creative
and the screwball.
So we must suffer the screwball gladly."
  - Kingman Brewster

The Art of Never Looking Back

By its very nature, being at the leading edge, pioneering, and being creative means taking risks and making lots of mistakes, being wrong a lot, and having your foot in your mouth from time to time. It's one of the dangers of being creative. Being a leader, at the head of the line, means once in awhile taking the wrong trail. Use these failures as stepping stones, don't look back and dwell on your failures... look back only to learn from them.

Most people will envy your creativity and remember only the good things you do rather than remembering your mistakes. If they remember your mistakes once in a while, that's all right too. It helps you keep your feet on the ground. Most people want to share in your creativity when you are successful. They want the association with your success.

It's not failure which blocks creativity, it's giving up when you fail... not recognizing that failure is a necessary part of success.

> *"Creativity is so delicate a flower*
> *that praise tends to make it bloom,*
> *while discouragement often nips it in the bud.*
> *Any of us will put out more and better ideas*
> *if our efforts are appreciated."*
> \- Alex F. Osborn

Managing Your Creativity and That of Others

Once you have discovered that it's okay to be creative, that creativity lends a zest to your life, and you have learned how to manage your own ideas, giving up your fears of risk and the fears of being identified as a "creative person," then you must try to share your knowledge with others. In light of what you know or have learned about your own creative abilities, I challenge you to share it with others, encouraging them, and allowing others to react and respond in the same ways that you yourself have mastered.

Learning how not to be throttled or stymied, means now insuring that others are not.

As our creative spirit grows and we look towards new frontiers we realize that nothing is ever finished. The joy comes from working, in perfecting our ideas, our projects, and our lives.

"A creative artist works on his next composition because he was not satisfied with his previous one."
                                    - Dimitri Shostakovich

Finally, you will only see the giants in the clouds if you look for them. Simple to say, but the first and perhaps most important rule of creativity is,
    you won't discover your creativity
    unless you look for it.

Lou Shaup
PMA Power
P.O. Box 1563
Rancho Cucamonga, CA 91730
(714) 987-8100

Lou Shaup

Lou Shaup is the owner and founder of PMA Power, which specializes in business and education consulting; career, academic and personal counseling, and public speaking.

Lou gives morale boosting talks to businesses, organizations, associations and schools, and teaches children and teenagers how to be peer helpers. He leads workshops and counsels people on careers, personal growth, academics and concerns or problems they face in everyday life situations, such as relationships, divorce, substance abuse, suicide prevention, etc. He also publishes "Fuel for Thought," a monthly newsletter of positive thoughts for positive thinkers.

Lou has written several articles for national and local publications, and has been on radio talk shows discussing issues concerning youth. In addition he has conducted workshops for state and local organizations.

He belongs to the American and California Associations of Counseling and Development, American and California School Counselors Associations, Positive Thinkers Club, National Employment Counselors Association, National Career Development Association, International Customer Service Association, and others.

Prior to owning his own business, Lou was a corporation executive. He has earned both B.S. and M.S. degrees from the University of LaVerne. He is married, has two children— a son and a daughter— and resides in Rancho Cucamonga.

The PMA* Principle
or, How a Sting Helped Me
Find My Potential

By Lou Shaup

*"The journey of a thousand miles
begins with one small step."*
                    - Lao-Tse

SUCCESS and HAPPINESS — All of us seek it, yet few achieve it, because we allow outside influences to dictate to us, when we should be looking within. SUCCESS — seven letters that have created a magazine; seven letters that have put people on a pedestal;

* Positive Mental Attitude

seven letters that have created good and bad in people. Let me put SUCCESS in perspective by quoting H. G. Wells:

"Wealth, notoriety, place and power are no measure of success whatever. The only true measure of success is the ratio between what we might have done and what we might have been on the one hand and the thing we have made and the thing we have made of ourselves on the other."

SUCCESS has nothing to do with materialistic wealth, titles or degrees we hold or our status in life. *It has to do with you, for who you are as a person is what really counts.* When God made you, he broke the mold. There will never be another just like you in this world, so why not become the best you that you can be. What counts most about SUCCESS is how a person achieves it.

Dare to beat your best! Don't compete with the whole world! Compete within yourself! SUCCESS and true HAPPINESS come from within a person. You can't buy it; you can't wish it upon yourself; you can't be given it by others. You have to earn it by being part of the human race and by helping others along life's path.

We were given life; it is our responsibility to give it purpose. Life is not accountable to you; you are accountable to life. Life is the greatest gift of all, yet most of us take it for granted. We all have God-given talents that are just waiting to be used; unfortunately, we put dollar and materialistic wealth before true happiness and success. Health is wealth. Without good health we have nothing.

It is not possible to be negative and depressed when you are doing something for others. I get my greatest satisfaction when I give of myself and help others. All of us need to learn to enjoy the beauty around us and within us.

I have achieved many goals in my life and want to share some of my accomplishments with you. Hopefully it will inspire you, so you can share it with others.

As I think of the goals I have achieved in life, I realize that the best is yet to come. This allows me to put life into perspective. There is a great future ahead, not just for me, but for everyone who is willing to make the effort to bring out their best.

I share my story hoping that it will inspire you to find your true potential and to become the best you that you can possibly be.

Tomorrow Will Be Even Better

I was born and raised in northeastern Pennsylvania. I have two of the greatest parents that anyone could ever have. What Mom and Dad lacked in formal education, they made up for by caring and sharing with others. My brother (Jim) and I grew up in a very supportive environment. We had our ups and downs during the growing up years, but Mom in her true God-given wisdom, always encouraged us. She told us, "Tomorrow will be even better than today."

Jim and I had the opportunity of growing up in a small town of approximately 500 people. The economy was mainly mining, railroads and agriculture. The area was surrounded by woods, providing a natural training and learning environment. When we camped out, we literally slept under the stars on a piece of canvas with a poncho and blanket as cover— no campers or sleeping bags for us.

In those days welfare was not prevalent, and the food put on our table was to be shared with those less fortunate than ourselves. I can remember Jim and I taking plates to other folks in our town. The thank you we received was enough to make us feel good the whole day.

A Stinging Challenge

As a student, there is nothing spectacular to tell. I was considered an average student (whatever that means), although I really enjoyed high school. I was a very shy, introverted person. Two things happened in high school that changed my life for the better.

During my last year in high school the drama teacher encouraged me to try out for the senior play. To my surprise I landed the lead part. I really felt good about myself and proud of my accomplishment. The play went very well and received rave reviews.

All who participated were pleased with the outcome and came away with a great sense of achievement. *I began to be me and, most importantly, to believe in myself.*

One day about three months before graduation something happened that changed my life forever. Until then I had been cruising through life not concerning myself too much one way or another with what I wanted to do in life. We were finishing up the school day in homeroom, and everyone was supposed to be studying or doing homework. Not me. I was clowning around, talking and bothering others.

Suddenly the teacher stood up, came to the front of her desk, and proceeded to let me have a verbal barrage saying, "Louis, all you ever do is fool around, when I know you could be doing better in school. You keep going the way you are, acting like a clown, not caring, and you will never amount to anything." After listening to this stinging criticism, I jumped to my feet and said, "You're wrong! Look around the room. I will make something of myself and become better than anyone here!" After having made my statement, embarrassment took over. My face turned beet red as I sat down and slouched in my seat. All the teacher did was smile, turn around, and return to her chair. After she sat down she continued to look at me with a smile on her face. This made me more irritated, and as I stewed there in silence, I began to realize that I'd really stuck my foot in my mouth.

On the way home on the school bus, besides the razzing from my classmates, I began to realize that it was the first time I ever really committed myself to anything. This was a turning point in my life, although I did not realize it at the time.

Shortly after graduation I joined the army, serving three years with a tour of duty in Vietnam, when few knew where the country was. I learned in Vietnam how fragile, yet precious, life is. I lost a very close friend there. When I went to Bien Hoa Air Force Base for the eulogy, there in front of me were eight aluminum caskets with an American flag draped over each one. A chaplain was speaking, but I do not remember much of what he said except at the end. What he said struck me like a bolt of lightening: "No young man should die without fulfilling his boyhood dreams." I made a vow to God right then and there that if I got out of Vietnam alive and whole, I owed him one.

Finding My Potential

Well, I did get out alive and whole, but somewhere I forgot my commitment, at least I thought so. But, He didn't. When my tour of duty ended and I was honorably discharged, I re-entered civilian life with no idea of what I was going to do—no focus.

While seeking employment, I remembered what the teacher said to me my senior year of high school. What she said made a lot of sense. She was saying, *you have potential, but the way you are going you will never find it.*

Set a Goal

My first job was doing warehouse work. My supervisor suggested I consider attending college. My comment was that my parents never had the opportunity to finish school, and going to college was beyond my abilities (or so I thought). That night in my apartment while listening to music and reading, the thought of college crossed my mind. I took a pencil and paper and wrote down, "To earn a college degree." I did not realize it at the time, but this was to become an important career and personal goal for me. I folded the paper and put it in my wallet. The next day at work I took the paper from my wallet and looked at it for quite a while, considering the possibilities. Some days later I asked my supervisor for the telephone number of his counselor at the college. I called and made an appointment for that same day.

My meeting with the counselor went well, and I sent for my high school transcripts. After receiving my transcripts, we met again to discuss my admission to college. After much discussion about me, my grades and my ability to handle college level classes, he said he would allow me to be accepted on probation. We looked at each other for what seemed a long time awaiting my decision. I finally spoke up and said, "You're on." He strongly advised me to start with a course in English and either sociology or psychology — not my favorite subjects. In addition, he said that I must get A's in the two subjects to stay in school and

get off probation. He assisted me in filling out the registration forms, and I paid the tuition charges. I was asking myself: What next? Why am I doing this? I was questioning whether I could really do this.

At home that night I pulled out the piece of paper with my goal and began to think of what must be done to earn a college degree. I listed some steps that I must achieve to reach my ultimate objective. The final thing I wrote on the piece of paper was a date to achieve the degree. When doubt crossed my mind, I remembered what my homeroom teacher had said.

That first semester was really tough going for me. I didn't realize how ill prepared I was for college. I struggled knowing I needed an A in each class to stay in school. The pressure was on and I accepted the challenge. Deep down my potential began to show itself. The next time I went to see the counselor, he had a big smile on his face. I said to him, "You didn't tell me I only needed a 2.0 grade point average (C grades) to stay in school and get off probation." He responded, "I knew it, but YOU didn't at the time. What if I had told you that you only needed a C average?" *He had challenged me and I had accepted the challenge, bringing out my best and filling myself with self-confidence, stamina and determination to achieve the objective.*

By the way, I set a six year time frame to earn a college degree. That did not happen, nor did it happen in ten or fifteen years. After twenty years, I earned a Bachelor of Science degree in Business Administra-

tion. Was I proud! Not only of myself but of those who had faith in me, and supported and encouraged me when I was ready to quit. This is the reason I now say: It is always too soon to quit, and never-never-never give up!

> *"Be not afraid of going slowly;*
> *be afraid only of standing still!"*
> - Chinese Proverb

Use the V-I-A Technique

What kept me going? My first year in college I attended graduation ceremonies to see what took place. I then began a *visualization* process that allowed me to see myself shaking a university official's hand as I received my degree. When I actually walked up on that stage and received my diploma, it was just like I had visualized it twenty years before.

After visualizing, I *internalized* my objective deep down inside. I planted the seed and then fertilized the seed with positive self-talk and positive self- expectations. This kept me going when the going got tough.

I then began the *actualization* process, which was doing what had to be done to earn my college degree.

Along the way came marriage, job transfers, and the birth of two children — additional challenges.

More importantly they were positive influences, because the job transfers were promotions and growth in my professional life, while my marriage and family were positive influences in my personal life, helping me to balance my responsibilities. Since the undergraduate degree, I have also earned a Master of Science degree in School Counseling.

Find a Purpose

Along with this, I started to realize that God has a mission in life for me—to help others achieve true success and happiness in their personal and professional lives.

Almost five years ago another goal became a reality, when I established my own business which is built upon the principle that it is in giving that we receive. I give morale boosting talks to businesses, organizations, associations and schools, teach children and teenagers how to be peer helpers, and spend time counseling people on careers, personal growth, academics and concerns/problems they face in everyday life situations, such as relationships, divorce, substance abuse, suicide prevention, etc. I now know what God-given talents I have and the mission in life God has assigned me.

Make Things Happen

I tell this story because it is about a person who was always under the impression that he was average. I let myself believe that...until I told my homeroom teacher that I would amount to something. It was many years later that I realized what that meant to me and my self-esteem. I also realize that I am a very positive person and my attitude shows it. I will always be thankful to that homeroom teacher, because she helped make a difference in my life. *It is never too late to change. You can either make things happen or let things happen! The choice is yours to make.*

I have become a firm believer in setting goals, putting them in writing, and then utilizing the V-I-A technique to achieve them. I can honestly state that any realistic goal that I have ever put in writing, and established steps and a flexible time frame in which to achieve it, I have either achieved or am now in the process of achieving.

My daily goal is simply this: To help another human being become a bigger and better person because I'll make them glad that they met me today.

Take a Risk

Opportunities come to those who seek. Nothing is gained in this world unless someone sets a goal and then works toward its achievement. Once meaningful goals are established, you will enjoy life more, then happiness (and no doubt prosperity if you want it) will become real.

You are in control of your life and you are responsible for your ultimate success or failure in whatever you do. Goals will help you establish priorities and control your life. Set goals for yourself and no one else. Don't let others control your destiny! *You are in charge!* Only you can determine what is best for you. Here again is the **V-I-A** technique:

1. Visualize - See it happening before the achievement actually takes place. A very powerful tool for goal achievement! I shared with you earlier my visualizing how I would receive my college degree.

2. Internalize - Make the commitment to pay the price for achievement. Establish a never-give-up attitude. Have the desire, persistence, determination, stamina, etc., to see it through.

3. Actualize - Make it happen. Every step forward leads you to achieving the goal(s) that others told you were impossible. Review each day the goal and the objectives that you established for achievement. Set a target date, be flexible, and reward yourself along the way.

How to Set Your Goals

State clearly and specifically in writing a goal(s) you would like to achieve in the next six months.

The following are some questions to consider when setting a goal:

1. Why do you want to achieve it?
2. If you succeed, what will it do for you?
3. What will you consider to be a moderate success? A good success? A tremendous success? Be specific.
4. How much do you want to achieve this goal?
5. How will achieving this goal contribute to the attainment of longer-range goals?
6. What price will you have to pay to achieve this goal? Are you willing to pay it?
7. Estimate your chances of achieving this goal.
8. What will happen if you aren't successful?
9. List the major subgoals involved in achieving this goal and assign a target date to each.
10. What obstacles stand between you and successful completion of this project? How will you overcome them?
11. What can you do today that will start you on the path to achieving this goal?

Attitude Makes the Difference

You must understand that you are somebody. You have a purpose in life. You are going somewhere. Use the power of a positive mental attitude (PMA) to generate positive results.

In a great country such as ours where opportunities abound, I have a hard time understanding why a person chooses a negative attitude over a positive one. Those who succeed in life have outstanding PMA's and high self-esteem. Every person has it within him/ herself to succeed.

The following ten steps can lead you to a more joyful and enthusiastic life:

1. Stop depreciating yourself.
2. Eliminate self-pity thoughts.
3. Quit thinking constantly of yourself. Think of others.
4. Use your God-given will power to do good.
5. Have a goal and put an achievable time table on it.
6. Think constructively. Quit griping about what might have been. The past is past. Think about what to do now.
7. Wake up every day thanking the good Lord that you are alive. Start the day asking for his guidance and counsel, so you can help others along the path of life.

8. Think and practice joy every day.
9. Get enthusiasm; think enthusiasm; live enthusiastically.
10. Think positive; get positive results.

As a closing comment, I share with you "The Secret of Life":

There is an old story about God discussing with his angels where he should place the Secret of Life so that it would be most difficult to find. One suggested the bowels of the earth; another the bottom of the sea; a third the highest mountain. A fourth angel objected, "Men will eventually search out all these places. The only place is within man himself. He will never dream of looking there."

This simple, short story is life itself. You must find from within the secret of life. For me, it is my PMA principle. Once you've found the secret of life, then you can achieve success and true happiness.

It's that simple.

*"What lies behind us and what lies before us
are small matters compared to what lies within us."*
- Ralph Waldo Emerson

**Dottie Walters with Dr. Yoshiro NakaMats,
the "Edison of Japan"**

Dottie Walters, C.S.P.
Royal Publishing, Inc.
18825 Hicrest Road
P.O. Box 1120
Glendora, CA 91740
(818) 335-8069

Dorothy M. Walters, C.S.P.

Dottie Walters is unique. She began her long and illustrious career with no car, one rickety stroller, two babies, a borrowed typewriter and a high school education. There were no jobs. The country was in a recession when Dottie started down the long road. She put cardboard in her shoes and kicked the wheel back on the stroller each time it came off.

Today Dottie is a World Class speaker, president of her International Speakers Bureau and publisher of the largest newsmagazine in the world of speakers, Sharing Ideas. *She has been honored three times by the National Speakers Association, with the Certified Speaking Professional designation, one of the first four United States women to receive it. She is a founding member of NSA, as well as the founding member of the Greater Los Angeles NSA Chapter. She founded the International Group of Agents and Bureaus and is Chairman of the Board of the American Association of Professional Consultants. She has initiated and sold several businesses, all based on advertising and publishing.*

She is currently president of four corporations, is an author, poet, speaker, seminar leader and publisher of anthologies featuring outstanding speakers. She has been fearuted in many TV and radio shows, newspaper and magazine articles, books and cassettes worldwide. Her first book, Never Underestimate the Selling Power of a Woman *is in its 15th edition.*

Dottie and Bob Walters have three children; an attorney, a speech and communication teacher, and the manager of their International Speakers Bureau.

The Spirit of Creativity

By Dottie Walters

*"To see a world in a grain of sand,
And a heaven in a wild flower,
Hold infinity in the palm of your hand,
And eternity in an hour."*
- William Blake

All creative things have the same elements in common. Dr. Yoshiro NakaMats of Toyko, the great inventor, told me, "Creativity begins with the spirit." What kind of spirit? An open and receiving one.

Today's professional speakers are the epitome of all the creative arts. They conceive the idea of their programs, write their own scripts, then perform. They market their programs to speakers bureaus and clients. They are Impresarios of their lives. Where does a professional speaker find the spark which ignites a worldwide speaking career?

A speaker's creativity is sparked by the inspiration of other speakers. Perhaps this has happened to you. Think of your favorite speaker, the best you have ever heard. Perhaps it was years ago that you sat in their audience, but you never have forgotten their message. Great speakers use stories to dramatize their points. Dr. Charles Jarvis, the funny dentist, is unforgettable with his famous bird story, Ken Mc Farland told his hilarious placque factory tale for banquets. Jesus of Nazarath gave us his story of the Good Samaritan. All used creative stories to insure their never-to-be-forgotten messages.

Every figure in history used this system. Aesop with his story of the tortoise and the hare is remembered because he used a creative idea to illustrate a great human lesson, "don't give up." His story of the fox and the grapes illustrates the point that we must not grouse that the grapes are not sweet, but instead take jumping lessons.

Diogenes used a lamp both on and off the stage to dramatize his "Search for Honesty." Creative storytelling speakers are those who are remembered. They "call out" our hearts, and our hopes.

Rev. Bob Richards, an Olympic champion, spoke at thousands of high schools. He called out to the young people, "I see someone in this audience who will be an Olympic Champion. That person knows who they are! That person is willing to pay the price for victory." Bob never completed a speech that he was not surrounded by young people shouting to him, "It is ME!"

When you sit in an audience and feel that pull to your heart, you are filled with a great spirit. You say to yourself, "I will be a speaker too." I will change peoples' lives. I will bring them laughter and hope and new ideas. That moment of creativity is called "Elation." The word comes from Greek roots. It literally means to "raise, or lift up." Einstein called it the "leap up of the mind." A moment before the idea is not there. Then suddenly like the flick of a TV switch, there is a great vision on the screen of our mind.

When a creative idea hits them, some people actually grab their heads. Have you done this, almost in surprise? Did you yell, "I got an idea!" Actually you did not get the idea. It got you. You were open, ready, receptive. The genius river flows through all of us. But some of us build dams against it, shutting its flood gates.

When you are inspired, the uplifting creative spirit surges in your mind like the waters of a geyser. It starts low, then flies higher and higher. That kind of joy comes from positive inspiration (another interesting word which literally means in-spirit-action). It never comes from the hurt or defeat of a rival. It comes pounding up from the hidden resources of our own souls in response to a great inspirational trigger. That trigger is often a speaker who tells a marvelous story.

Sometimes inspiration is delayed. The inspirational story of the speaker is keyboarded into our unconscious mind to reside "in memory." Then when we are in trouble or jeopardy, when we are stressed and hurting, we have a dream. Sometimes an awake one, sometimes a sleeping one. Our unconscious brings up the message of hope and plays it back for us. Charles Lindberg told of hearing voices from history whispering encouragement in his ears as he flew his tiny plane all alone over the dark Atlantic Ocean to France.

Creativity in Dreams

Herbert Trench wrote this about inspiration:

> *"She comes not when Noon is on the roses*
> *Too bright is Day.*
> *She comes not to the soul 'till it reposes*
> *From work and play*
> *But when night is on the hills, and the great Voices*
> *Roll in from Sea,*
> *By starlight and by candlelight and dreamlight*
> *Inspiration comes to me."*

Often the genius river projects creative dream pictures of the future. When I was a little girl, I dreamed repeatedly of standing on a large stage, speaking. No one in my family was a speaker or a writer. There were no Billy Grahams, William Jenning Bryans or Aimee Semple McPhersons in my family.

In my dream, I stood with my arms outstretched and spoke with all my heart. I had a great message to give to my audience. My voice rose and fell with earnestness. Tears were in my eyes. The people leaned forward to hear me. But I could not under-stand my own words. I kept waking to think, "What is it I must say?"

That mysterious dream of a poor little girl with a very difficult life actually came true, and in the most unusual way. When it happened, I learned the miss-ing part of the dream, my message. I now have actually stepped out on thousands of platforms and stages in front of audiences of 2,000 and 4,000, and rallies before as many as 14,000 people. My heart pounded, my mouth was dry, but my nervousness left me as I picked up the mike. A wonder came over me that the lectern, lights, and the faces before me were familiar and dear. I knew them from my repeated dreams.

Psychologist Victor Frankel told the same kind of story. He was incarcerated in a Nazi Prison camp. All around him prisoners gave up, and died. He dreamed of telling his story before vast audiences. He wanted to explain what he learned in that camp. His message would be that it truly is more blessed to give than to receive. He always took part of his meager meal and gave it to a prisoner who was in despair. He talked to them of hope. He lifted up their spirits, and in so doing, he lifted himself up. The spirit of giving love was the one thing the Nazis could not take from him.

Victor Frankel lived, and did speak to huge audiences. He told them all he had been with them before. He knew them from his dreams.

The Prophetic Dream

Here is the story of how that repeated dream of mine came true, and how I came to speak on world platforms with Dr. Norman Vincent Peale, Gov. George Romney, Rev. Robert Schuller, Zig Ziglar and hundreds of other famous speakers in auditoriums all the way from London to Malasia. It happened because of stress and trouble.

My father abandonded us when I was 13. There had never been any money if I wanted something. So I sold bouquets of wild flowers, or gathered bottles to take back to the grocer to collect the pennies. I even figured out how to buy a five cent ice milk cone that came in 4 scoops, and sell the other kids licks for a penny a piece.

In high school I got a job in the bakery of a midnight market. I worked from 3 to midnight and all day Saturday and Sunday. My check helped my mother. My English teacher had pulled me out of English class and insisted I take journalism. I caught fire. After the cases and trays were washed and the floor swept, it got quiet in the midnight market. I leaned on the counter and wrote stories, poems and articles on the bakery bags for our "Alhambra High Moor" newspaper. When I was creating ideas, the minutes flew by in that cold drafty open air market. In journalism class our wonderful teacher inspired us all to want to be writers. I dreamed of going to the Journalism School at the University of Missouri, which she said was the best in the country.

But instead I went to work the day after graduation and gave my mother my checks. I found a quotation by Amelia Earhart at the library that I carried with me and read every day. She was a great creative genius who followed her dream into the sky. She said,

> "Some of us have runways built for us.
> If you do, take off. But if you don't, know that it is
> your responsibility to grab a shovel.
> Your job is that of dreamer, architect, builder."

When my sweetheart, Bob Walters, came home from the war we married and had two babies. We bought a little tract home, furniture, a small dry cleaning business, a car. We were deeply in debt. Then recession struck. The dry cleaning business failed.

We could not make any of the payments. Our little home was four miles from town. I was worried sick. We would soon lose our home, everything. Then I had that dream of speaking again.

When I woke, I thought, "There is that crazy dream! Speaking is no solution!" Then suddenly I saw in my mind's eye my high school journalism teacher who spoke to us in such an exciting way about creativity. She taught us, "A moment's insight is sometimes worth a life's experience," as Oliver Wendell Holmes said. I got an idea.

I sat up all night typing up that idea on an old battered typewritter I borrowed. It was a "shoppers column" of small paragraphs featuring my own homemaker's reaction to the services and goods offered in our town. I used the ideas in the ads to write the column.

Bob needed the car, but I did have a baby stroller. I stuck a pillow in the back of it to make a 2nd seat, put both children in and trudged the long, hot dusty road to town and the newspaper office. The stroller was so heavy, one wheel kept coming off. I slipped my shoe off and hit the wheel back on with the heel every few feet. I was uplifted with a strong spirit of being on a great life path. It was a feeling of pro-motion. Positive active action.

I found the Baldwin Park Bulletin office and pushed open the heavy door. The woman at the counter sounded depressed. "No, there are no jobs here. It is August. We are laying people off work. Don't you know there is a recession going on? If you do sell ads in this town you can't collect for them. No one has any money. There is no chance for you!" One of my babies started crying.

Light the Lights!

Suddenly I felt as if someone had put a spotlight on me. I turned and smiled at her. "I am sorry. I did not come for a job," I explained. "I am here to buy advertising space at wholesale. I will sell the spaces to the merchants of the town at retail. My column will be a paid feature for your newspaper. Your readers will love it, and you will make money on it."

She gasped. Then she called the publisher out of his office to talk to me. I used all the newspaper jargon my journalism teacher had taught us. I showed him my sample column, asked for a special spot in the newspaper, and promised to get my copy in early. He agreed to everything. Then I took a deep breath and asked them to let me have the first week on credit. That column cost $20.00 at wholesale. If I sold all the ads to fill it, I could collect $40.00. Four weeks of $20 profit each would make the $80 house payment. It was a deal. I began.

Curtain Up!

Then the strange dream of speaking began to come true. I noticed that the Baldwin Park Bulletin ran stories of local clubs who featured speakers. Rotary, Kiwanis, Soroptomist, the Chamber of Commerce. I saw that the members of these clubs were the very merchants I wanted to sell my shoppers' column ads to. I decided that I would speak to them! The minute that idea came into my head, it was as if someone had plugged in an electric light. It was a warm friendly spotlight like the one I thought I was standing in at the newspaper office .

I thought of what those prospects, those business people, would like to hear. The creativity light in my mind flashed. I wrote down, "What Does Your Customer Really Want?" as my title.

Then I began phoning the clubs to offer myself as their speaker. My neighbor agreed to take care of my babies for the hour I would be gone to speak, and to loan me her car. I babysat her children in exchange. Three of the clubs booked me right away. I took along copies of my newspaper, marking my column with green crayola. I thought, "green for GO!" I placed a copy at each place at the luncheon tables.

I remembered reading somewhere that it takes "a big smile to open the doors, and a little money to grease the wheels." So I bought a pen for a prize. I took a little flower decorated basket with me and asked my audience for their business cards for a drawing. The next day I called all of the merchants from the cards, and sold my column ads over the telephone. No more rickety stroller! I began to pay off the debts.

If a merchant did not have cash, I traded my advertising space for the things I needed. A used car, upholstery for it, groceries.

Opening Doors

One day, as I spoke to a local service club, one of the merchants came up and asked me to talk to him about an idea he had, a newcomer welcoming business. He suggested that I call on new residents and deliver to them civic information and coupons from his business and other businesses. Each business would pay me $20 a month for 50 home calls.

The light flashed in my mind again. I agreed to organize the business. I soon had 40 businesses signed up, including my newspaper publisher. We solicited subscriptions for him. $800 a month was a whole lot of money. I hired my neighbors to help me. Soon the welcoming business was so large I had to give up the newspaper column.

We called it Hospitality Hostess. It grew to 250 cities in Southern California, with 4,000 retail merchants and 225 employees in 4 offices. In each area I used my talk to the local clubs to open the district and to promote sales. We became the biggest welcoming service in the West, with many large advertisers who used us in all of the cities we covered.

Then one day at one of my talks, one of the merchants came to me and asked me if I would speak to his employees on customer relations. He offered me $50. A fortune! That speech opened the doors to my speaking all over the United States, Canada, England, Australia, and Malasia. The scene in my dreams became reality!

When You Open a Mind—
It Cannot Be Closed Again

Creativity is like a string of flashing lights. When one is ignited it sets off the next, then the next. I decided that since I had no college education, I must educate myself. Amelia Earhart was right. My responsibility was to be the builder, but I needed tools. So I went to the public library and picked up stacks of biographies of the achievers of the world.

Fortunately my mother had often left me at the children's room of the public library when I was little, as she could not afford a baby sitter. I was an only child but I grew up with books. I read my way around the children's room, then the junior room, then upstairs where I met Voltaire, and Ben Franklin and Plato. For me, the library was full of voices. All friendly, smiling, waiting for me like a giant family with outstretched arms. They never yelled at me or scolded me. I took my books to bed with me every night.

For Us

Once, years later as I spoke to a large audience in Denver, Colorado, I told of reading every book our little library offered on sales, creativity and business. A book that especially helped me was Charles Roth's

Secrets of Closing Sales. I said that I thought he and the other authors wrote their books especially for me, because I needed them so.

I explained that I could hear his voice in the pages of his book saying, "Don't give up, Dottie. Think of a new creative idea. Think of a better way. *Think!*"

At that moment a man in the back of the room jumped up and ran to the stage. He raced up the stairs and embraced me. I was astounded.

"I am Charles Roth!" he shouted. "Yes, Dottie Walters! I did write that book just for you. Every writer, every speaker creates for the longing, listening, thirsty heart."

One of the books at the library was about a brilliant woman, Madam de Stael. I could hear her voice as she told me, "I would walk five hundred miles to talk to, or learn from, a person of genius." I saw advertisements of wonderful speakers who were coming to Los Angeles. I went to hear them. Bruce Barton, the magnificient advertisng man was one of them. I sat in awe as he spoke. I was so inspired, so lifted up.

I waited until he was finished and all of the other people had taken his hand and thanked him. I was the last one. I looked into his eyes and said, "I heard you!" He took my hand very kindly and said, *"You are the one I came for."*

Creativity at Home

I always read stories to my children. We still trade books, discuss them, enjoy them together. When they were little, we loved to play creativity games we invented. One we called "Heads Up!" I would set the stage, telling of someone with a problem. Then each of us would think of solutions. Could it be made bigger, smaller, could they combine it with something else. As idea struck against idea, their eyes would open to more and more solutions.

"There is never just one way to solve a problem," I taught them. We formed a family "Brain Trust." When they grew older and had problems of their own, it was so easy for us to get together and have a "Heads Up!" session. Another game was with the many quotation books I constantly bought. I read the quotation to them, without reading the name of the author. Then we would discuss what era it might have come from. What was going on at that time? What kind of person would say this? Did we agree with the philosophy or not?

Then they would guess who said it. One of my favorites is from the inspirational teacher of Confucius, Lao Tsze: "To see things in the seed, that is genius." Soon the children could recognize the ideas of Plato, Franklin, Tom Edison, Florence Nightingale and many more friends of the mind. I remember that my daughter loved Florence's "We are ready! Send my nurses to the Crimea!" She created modern nursing. None existed before Florence saw the vision of what could be.

We talked about Robert Goddard, the father of modern Rocketry. Without his inventions and experiments there would be no space program. I told the children the story of how Robert climbed the cherry tree in his backyard when he was thirteen. He had been ill for a long time. It was his first day to be allowed outside. He had read all of the science fiction stories of his time — Jules Verne, H.G. Wells. He sat in the sunshine in the limbs of his favorite tree. Suddenly he looked down at the ground and saw a space vehicle, a rocket. No such ship existed. He stayed there several hours studying every detail of it.

Finally he climbed down and asked his mother for a note book. In it he sketched what he had seen. He recorded every rocket experiment he ever made in that book. We discussed a man named Strause who could not figure out how to build the San Francisco Bay bridge until he saw the idea of suspension in a dream.

The Message in the Dream

What was the message that little girl tried so hard to tell to her phantom audience in her dreams? I found it. It is the source of genius. Genius is not a person. Not you or me. It is the powerful creative force. The river of creative ideas, ever flowing, ever gushing.

The dictionary defines it as a "spring in which there is always more behind, than flows forth."

My message is that we must listen to the people of accomplishment and creativity like Dr. NakaMats. We must associate with people who are engineers and dreamers and planners and visionaries. We must seek them out. We can recognize them because they are the ones who create, combine, change, amplify and animate. They are the ones who ignore the dunces of the world who sit back and criticize. They are the ones who often pretend they are deaf to negative thinkers, as Tom Edison did.

Listening to people of accomplishment, those who solve old problems and create new combinations to better our world is like setting dynamite. The clog is blown away in a flash. Ideas flow ever faster. The genius river floods over adversity, stress, and problems which in reality are only temporary setbacks to the stream of genius.

As my friend of the mind, Albert Einstein told me,

"Talent trickles; genius is a flash flood."

"You can count the number of seeds in an apple,
but who can count the number of apples in a single seed?"
- Dr. Herb True, University of Notre Dame

I am convinced that when I meet my Maker,
the query will not be:

"Why were you not more like this one or that one?"

No, the Divine question will be:

"Why did you not dream, listen, and love more?

Why did you not create, give and inspire more?

*Why did you not use every precious moment
I gave you?*

*Why were you not more like the great, strong person
I envisioned when you were conceived?*

For I made only one of you."

– Dottie Walters